ADVANCE PRAISE

"This book is the missing piece in your growth strategy. While most teams stay focused on surface-level tweaks, Talia gets to the heart of what actually drives conversions: emotion. There's no one better to show you how emotion drives sustainable growth."
—Dave Gerhardt, Founder Exit Five, Former CMO

"Everyone says emotional marketing works. But few (like... very, very, very few) can show you how to do it — step by step, with real examples, and the lived experience to back it up. In Emotional Targeting, Talia Wolf generously and brilliantly breaks it all down. This is the rare book that shows you how to build brand love and drive performance. Read it if you want your performance marketing to have more heart, and your brand marketing to have sharper KPIs." |
—Amanda Natividad, VP of Marketing at Sparktoro

"Talia doesn't just teach you how to boost conversions—she hands you the blueprint to your customer's heart. Emotional Targeting is the book I wish I read five years ago. Fewer 'best practices.' More best outcomes."
—Ross Simmonds, Author of Create Once, Distribute Forever

"Persuading prospects just got immensely easier, thanks to Emotional Targeting. Talia explains exactly what it takes to connect and convert. Keep her book nearby; it's that good."
—Nancy Harhut, Author, Using Behavioral Science in Marketing

"Finally, a guide teaching marketers how to use emotion for strategic advantage, rather than traditional CRO tactics that, frankly, don't work anymore. Talia's perspective as a CEO and CRO combine in Emotional Targeting to objectively teach a deeply human approach that really works!"
—Devin Bramhall, Growth Advisor

"While everyone's running on the optimization hamster wheel, Talia shows you how emotional targeting drives hockey-stick growth when traditional CRO hits a ceiling. Game-changer."
—Sean Ellis, Author of Hacking Growth

EMOTIONAL TARGETING

EMOTIONAL TARGETING

WIN HEARTS. BOOST SALES. OWN THE MARKET.

TALIA WOLF

EMOTION SELLS PRESS

Copyright © 2025 by Talia Wolf

All rights reserved. No portion of this book may be reproduced in any form without written permission from the publisher or author, except as permitted by applicable copyright law. This work is protected under Israeli copyright law and international copyright treaties, including the Berne Convention.

EMOTIONAL TARGETING
Win hearts. Boost sales. Own the market.

FIRST EDITION
ISBN 978-965-93251-1-5 (paperback)
ISBN 978-965-93251-0-8 (ebook)

Produced by Write & Main
www.writeandmain.com
Cover design by Talia Wolf & Jessica Noel

www.taliawolf.com

TABLE OF CONTENTS

Introduction:	How to tell if you should read this book	8
Chapter 1:	The deadly hamster wheel of optimization	14
Chapter 2:	How your customers actually decide what to buy	26
Chapter 3:	Introducing The Emotional Targeting Framework™	38
Chapter 4:	Emotional Targeting™ research — What it is and how to run it	52
Chapter 5:	Synthesizing your research	72
Chapter 6:	Running an Emotional Targeting™ Audit	84
Chapter 7:	Running meaningful tests	102
Chapter 8:	Bringing it home	114

INTRODUCTION

HOW TO TELL IF YOU SHOULD READ THIS BOOK

SUPERHEROES DON'T WIN BECAUSE OF THEIR POWERS, THEY WIN BECAUSE THEY KNOW WHO THEY'RE FIGHTING FOR. GREAT MARKETERS DO TOO.

"I need to drive more sign-ups. More demo requests. More sales opportunities."

I hear some version of this from every Head of Growth or VP of Marketing I speak to in every consulting session, workshop and sales call.

It's a universal problem — after all, driving more conversions is a major part of the job description. The challenge, of course, is that knowing what you need to do doesn't actually help you figure out how to go about it.

Every company — even those that seem to sell fairly identical products — is different. There are both big and subtle differences in how the solution is actually built, in the sub-problems it tends to focus on, in the way the user experience is shaped and in the ICPs this product is actually right for.

To meaningfully increase conversions, you need to understand these differences and understand how to position everything as strengths to your specific ICPs. *(Which is often easier said than done!)*

But... there is a way.

I wrote this book as a way to finally capture how GetUplift — the CRO agency I founded — helps high-growth companies consistently increase conversions, because the answer I give in those conversations is always a variation of the same core theme: **"Try emotional targeting."**

At its core, emotional targeting helps you understand what prospects are feeling when they're searching for a solution like yours and what they want to feel after they've bought and implemented it. When you understand this, you can optimize the entire buying experience so that it reflects those emotions back to your customers. In other words, you can show them you know exactly what they need, why they need it and why you are the smartest choice.

The more specific you can get, the better the results. This is all because of a simple truth that sometimes gets lost in our data- and tracking-obsessed field:

Decision making — especially at the highest levels — isn't as data-driven or as simple as it might appear.

A potent cocktail of cognitive biases and psychological triggers flows through the subconscious and subtly influences what you say yes and no to. It affects which results you pay attention to and which ones you choose to ignore. It nudges you towards one particular homepage headline over all the alternatives. It whispers in your ear when you're reviewing designs in Figma or analyzing and breaking down competitor brand strategy.

These biases and triggers work away in the background, unseen, and quietly drive the success or failure of businesses everywhere. This is true in B2C and it's true in B2B. The difference is that one side knows and embraces this fact, while the other side tries to hide from it.

A TALE AS OLD AS ADVERTISING

Emotional targeting has been a fundamental part of B2C marketing for decades. It's why cool celebs and influencers probably sell more shoes than just about anyone else. It's why one of the most iconic

Lego ads ever made has a grinning child showing off their latest creation. Lego figured out early on that no parent can resist a happy, smart, confident kid ready to take on the world and parents instantly bought into the bright, creative future they saw for their children. This ad is how Lego ousted Ferrari as the world's most powerful brand.[1]

And yet, despite all the success B2C brands have achieved, very few B2B brands optimize their marketing strategies for emotion. Instead, they optimize for features, awards or 'being number one,' as if a long shopping list of capabilities or saying they're the best in the business will make it easy for prospects to choose them. *(Or make it easy for those same prospects to justify that decision to an entire team of colleagues and managers while their professional reputation hangs in the balance!)*

Contrary to what some '80s managers seemed to believe, people don't check their personalities at the door and transform into number-crunching machines the second they take the elevator up to the office. Our personal biases and emotions are just as present at work as they're at home.

If you can understand and map out these emotions and biases and then connect them to specific points of the buying journey, you'll be unstoppable. You'll have the strategic key to unlocking what your customers need and consistently helping your team create experiences that meet those needs.

---

[1] https://www.theguardian.com/lifeandstyle/2017/jun/04/how-lego-clicked-the-super-brand-that-reinvented-itself

YOU ARE NOT A COMPUTER.
NEITHER ARE YOUR CUSTOMERS.

Back in 2013, Volvo spent between $3-4 million on their most iconic ad 'The Epic Split' with Van Damme and generated $170 million in revenue from a 75-seconds video.

Emotional triggers have to be a strategic part of any successful B2B marketing strategy that's designed to appeal to living, breathing, business decision-making humans. And when it is, magic actually happens.

I know this, because it's been my agency's 'secret sauce' for a decade. Optimizing for emotion helped us increase sign-ups by 54% for a project management solution competing in a crowded, highly competitive space where every solution had the same basic packet of features and accolades. And it helped us increase organic search conversions by 72.8% for a leading identity orchestration company that sells to major global enterprises in an extremely technical space.

All this was the result of smart research, analysis, user journey mapping and emotional targeting — a repeatable process we call The Emotional Targeting Framework™. **And in this book I'm going to take you through the science behind it and then show you you how to use it.**

So if you're being measured on your ability to drive more sign-ups, demos or sales and you want a strategic, easy-to-follow, repeatable process for getting there and nailing your KPIs and OKRs, then this is the book for you.

Let's begin.

CHAPTER 1

THE DEADLY HAMSTER WHEEL OF OPTIMIZATION

EVEN THE FLASH BURNS OUT WHEN HE RUNS IN CIRCLES.

I've worked with and trained hundreds of brands across B2B, SaaS and e-commerce since starting out in CRO back in 2013. While every business I've worked with has been unique, they all had the same problem: **brilliant products, frustrating conversion results.**

To better understand how to solve this wide-spread conversion problem, we at GetUplift had to understand WHY this was happening. What were these brands doing (or not doing) that kept them from the results they deserved?

The more experiments we ran, the more it became clear that almost every business tries to tackle their conversion problem the same way:

1) Leaning heavily on 'best practices'
2) Speaking to *too* broad an audience
3) Overcomplicating their funnels
4) Over-relying on software to fast-track their results

At a glance, these may look like four small mistakes. However, they are a core problem that keeps marketers on what I like to call 'the deadly hamster wheel of optimization'. Once you step on board, you find yourself endlessly chasing the conversion increase by looking for 'proven solutions' and trying to fix broken 'elements' on a page, going in never ending circles with no real results to show for your trouble.

No one ends up in the hamster wheel on purpose — it always starts out innocently enough. You check your reports and see that your conversions *still* aren't where they need to be. In a bid to improve them, you Google (or ask AI for) a few best practices, check out what the latest thought leader has recommended on Linkedin and start testing. Maybe you test a new CTA button, or fewer form fields, or more customer testimonials and bigger, better logos.

But for some reason, the recommended tests don't work as well on your funnel, so you turn to your competitors. Surely they know what they're doing, right? Everyone seems to have embraced the latest and greatest trends, so you try adding 'AI-powered,' 'the #1 solution for X' or 'the all-in-one solution' to your headline so you're not left behind. The frustrating result is that you end up with a site where, if you switched your logo out with your competitor's, no one would know the difference.

That's when you start throwing money at the problem. You invest in 'the best in breed' tools and software solutions – segmentation, AI, a better AB testing platform. You spend countless hours getting them installed and set up. And when you're ready to start using them to get real results, you go back to Google or your favorite AI and look for best practices… and the hamster wheel spins again

This wheel keeps spinning because most conversion optimization recommendations you'll find online are tactical, not strategic. They're founded on the concept of changing elements on a page until you manage to arrange everything in a magical order — instead of focusing on the underlying problem.

But to get the meaningful, repeatable results your business needs, you have to first understand the problem. So instead of skipping this chapter in a race to the solution, I encourage you to resist the temptation to say, "this doesn't apply to us," and get honest about what is and isn't working. Pay attention to how each mistake leads to the next so you can catch yourself making them before you get sucked back into the expensive cycle of guesswork, wondering what on earth to try next.

MISTAKE #1: YOU RELY ON 'BEST PRACTICES' OR COPY YOUR COMPETITORS... (*OR DO A BIT OF BOTH*)

We've all been guilty of clicking articles titled "Best Practices for B2B Pricing Pages," and "Top 15 homepages you should copy if you want to increase conversions today" hoping they'll solve our conversion problems. Usually, they tell you to include social proof, add a video to your hero section or scatter more CTA buttons all over the page... all without understanding the context of your website. And so you wind up changing random elements on the page, giving yourself a check for every change you make. These changes have no impact OR worst-case scenario, decrease conversions, so you end up back to the drawing board. In the best-case scenario, changing your button from red to blue increases conversions by <made up>%. But here's the problem... even if you achieved an uplift, you don't actually have a real understanding about why and how you got it. And without that, you can't repeat the experiment and get even higher uplifts. In short, you're left with no idea about what to do next.

Sadly, that's not the only problem. One of my biggest frustrations with best practices is that they're rarely rooted in reliable data. That post you read about the guru who increased signups by 300% simply by removing form fields looks pretty impressive... at first. But when you dig deeper, you realize he increased his conversions from one signup to four (nothing to pop champagne about). But let's give Mr. LinkedIn Guru the benefit of the doubt. Let's say he genuinely increased signups from 1000 to 4000 and they were all solid, qualified leads. Just because removing form fields increased *his* conversions doesn't mean you'll get the same results, because your customers are completely different. And so is your product. And your user journey.That's why these articles are annoying, misleading clickbait. (I should know... I used to write them #*guilty*.)

I love this example because I almost always see 'reduce form fields' come up when people talk about B2B best practices or 'surprising' tips and tricks. Maybe you've seen it too. Maybe you even tried it, seen a dramatic increase in your conversion rate and, after looking at the data, realized it led to crappy leads. Anyone and everyone was signing up and while you might have increased conversions, your entire sales team was frustrated because they were overwhelmed with unqualified leads. Someone else's best practice wound up screwing with your sales pipeline. *(This actually happened to a collegue...)*

And that's not even the worst of it. **The biggest problem with best practices is that they don't give you knowledge you can apply to the rest of your marketing strategy.** Knowing the exact shade of orange your competitor used to get more button clicks *(kudos Amazon!)* doesn't help *you* with what to say to your customers. Likewise, using a carousel, because that's what everyone else is doing, won't tell you which features your customers care about most. Not to mention the fact carousels drive many readers (myself included) nuts. Before you can absorb the information on the slide, it's already changed.

When it comes to finding the *right* messages (the ones that make your reader think, *"Finally! This is exactly what I need!"*), you must turn your attention away from what everyone else is doing and onto your audience's pains and challenges. You won't get those answers from best practice guides, or by opening up a bunch of tabs so you can hop between well-funded SaaS brands and then swipe what they're doing. You might *think* that your competitors have it all figured out, but chances are, their team is doing the same as you. It happens in every industry, and as a result, every website looks and feels exactly the same.

If you want to differentiate yourself from the competition and make it easy for your customers to differentiate *you*, you need a stronger strategy. Without one, you'll not only get frustrated when you look and sound like everyone else, but you'll find yourself falling into the next trap.

MISTAKE #2: YOU SPEAK TO EVERYONE

Thousands of sales messages bombard your audience every day. This means they've become masters of blocking out what doesn't apply to them — 99% of messages go straight to their internal 'spam' folder before their brains can even notice them.

Narrowing down your solution to a specific audience feels risky. It can feel like literally turning away revenue. We've all sat in meetings about our target audience, only to hear executives and colleagues say, "everyone's our audience," or "everyone can use it" – but this critical decision is what ends up diluting every single piece of marketing you put out there. From the emails you send to the ads and landing pages you create, by speaking to everyone, you end up speaking to no one. Your prospects land on your site, cannot for the life of them see how you're different from anyone else, and leave. By trying to please the biggest group, you're automatically sending yourself to spam along with the bazillion B2B companies out there saying the exact same thing.

To stand out, you must zero in on who you're selling to. You must **stop speaking to everyone and instead choose a specific problem you want to solve for a particular audience.** This is *especially* true if you're selling in a saturated market.

Emotional targeting case study: Project management tool increases organic conversions by 54% from their comparison page

It's no secret that project management tools operate in a packed, competitive market. The options are endless and they all offer the same basic solution: better project management. So when a leading PM solution asked GetUplift to help optimize a critical landing page designed to persuade prospects to choose them instead of their top competitor, we knew that sticking with generic messaging was going to do absolutely nothing.

To have a hope of optimizing the page to drive more trials, we had to understand:

1) What the brand's Ideal Customer Profile (ICP) specifically cared about when searching for a project management solution
2) What unique problems ICPs were trying to solve that their current solution couldn't help them with
3) What led customers to switch from the competitor to our client

4) Who was involved in the decision-making process and what priorities did they have that might influence the choice

To start answering these questions, we interviewed the client's ideal customers — agencies, creative teams and client-facing teams. During those interviews, we identified the three big elements that client-facing teams care about the most: they wanted a product that was built for *their* kind of work, they wanted proof that teams like theirs used this tool, and they wanted to know it would be easy to use so that their teams would actually adopt the solution

But customer interviews offer one side of the story. To understand the other side, we spoke to prospects who'd actively switched away from the competitor, and ran an in-depth competitor analysis. During that process, we discovered that even though the competitor looked cheaper initially, hidden upsells made it more expensive in the long run. On top of this, onboarding was tricky and relied on hiring someone to help — making adoption much harder and longer than it needed to be.

Once we understood the problems, the execution was simple. We crafted a page that focused on the specific pains and challenges client-serving teams face daily and clearly showed them where our client succeeded and the competitor failed.

This simple strategic approach led to **a 54% increase in free trial sign-ups from organic traffic.**

If you're worried that by speaking to a specific audience, you will alienate potential buyers who don't fit into that segment, then I have news for you: **you're already alienating your true customers**. The people you created the product for aren't buying because you're not speaking to them. Instead, your non-specific messaging is bringing in people who will not use your product. Those people are going to turn away at some point, but by failing to get specific about who you're talking to, you're losing customers who would buy and love your product, because they can't see how it would benefit them. In an attempt to win those customers back, you fall into the third trap.

MISTAKE #3: YOU OVERCOMPLICATE THINGS

Speaking to everyone comes with an unexpected side effect: over-compensation. To make up for the lack of specificity — just in case getting too specific pushes a certain segment away — too many brands lean into industry buzz-terms and overt repetition. The best messages start sounding too simple, generic or broad and so they get buried in long-winded pages designed to show just how great the product is for solving every problem in existence.

This isn't an argument against long-form copy. But to be effective, long pages have to have a distinct purpose and strategy behind them — the pages I'm talking about here tend to become long by accident. They pull together every 'high converting element' and then meander, jumping from one thought to another — features, pricing, features, pricing, irrelevant testimonials and so on. By trying to say everything, they confuse visitors and fail to convert them into free trial users, leads or buyers. Not because your product isn't awesome, but **because visitors are struggling to see what's in it for them**.

If your website reads like this, it's not your fault. You've probably been writing copy for all the customer profiles you were given, all at the same time. The problem is, there are too many personas that include too many industries. The team's been afraid to narrow the list down because *what if they narrow down to the wrong audience?*

By playing it 'safe' and keeping your audience broad, you end up talking about your product in ways that don't resonate with your best-fit customers. Prospects can see a bunch of technical features, **but they can't understand how your product fits into their everyday lives.** Because you haven't zoned in on a specific audience, you end up overcomplicating your offer, funnels and messaging. You don't know what's working and what's not, so you decide to throw money at the problem. Which brings us to...

MISTAKE #4: YOU USE TOOLS AND SOFTWARE TO FAST-TRACK YOUR RESULTS

By this point, you've tried swiping from your competitors and wound up sounding like everyone else and overcomplicating things. Your results aren't where you want them to be, so you're desperately scouring the internet and consulting with colleagues, trying to figure out what to optimize next (*random A/B test, anyone?*). Eventually, someone suggests that the right software will solve all your problems!

So, desperate and ready for this to be over, you get some new tech. But plastering tools over a structural issue, is the online equivalent of painting your walls beige when your foundation is crumbling. Using "cutting-edge" software and tools without a proper strategy first, just takes you back to the start: googling best practices.

Each of these mistakes is keeping you on a never-ending wheel of guesswork. To make matters worse, everyone and their cat has an opinion on what you should be doing. You get an email from the CEO or highest paid person in the room (HIPPO) asking why you're not doing <unstrategic best practice> because <huge competitor> is doing it, so you should be too. Your executive team insists you highlight your product is powered by AI because they think talking more about the tech will solve the problem of what to say to your customers (it won't, trust me).

Segmentation, AI, heatmaps... using these tools as a crutch will keep you mediocre at best. They might tell you how much time users spend on the page, but they won't help you understand who your customers are or what's weighing on their minds. You're left with pretty graphs, but no meaningful knowledge you can use to grow the business. Without this knowledge, you're just standing in front of a prospect, asking them to love you. Something has to change.

Which brings us to emotional targeting — the smartest way to dial in your audience so you know exactly who you're selling to and what they need to hear to confidently convert.

Fair warning: your new (and improved) strategy will feel slower at first. Instead of zooming through tactics, you'll do the work of applying a long-term strategy that will inform decisions across your entire customer-facing business. The difference is, instead of going round and round in circles, you'll finally have a solid roadmap to follow. This difference is pivotal because while walking down Route 101 to San Francisco (i.e. doing the work of emotional *strategy*) might *feel* slower than racing around a hamster wheel, only one will get you where you need to go.

CHAPTER 2

HOW YOUR CUSTOMERS ACTUALLY DECIDE WHAT TO BUY

EVERY SUPERHERO HAS AN ORIGIN STORY. SO DOES EVERY PURCHASE DECISION.

Emotional Targeting drives sales for the biggest brands in the world.

Marketers have been using emotion in offline campaigns for decades to build connections and loyalty and grow revenue. Yet in the digital marketing world, where data and tracking dominate decision-making, leveraging emotion often takes a backseat. Messaging focuses on pricing and features, even though the biggest brands in the world — like Lego, Coca-Cola, and Apple — effectively use emotion in their advertising over and over.

Take Nike for example. Up until 2012, Nike mostly used mega stars and celebrities in their campaigns. The strategy was simple — potential buyers would see Michael Jordan wearing their new shoes and run to the stores. Everyone and their sister wanted to look and feel and play like Jordan, so of course they'd buy his shoes *(this isn't a unique strategy to Nike, all the big brands use it)*. But then, in 2012 Nike shattered their sales goals with their new emotion-based campaign.

What made this campaign so successful was the shift the company made in its emotional targeting strategy from *"buy and be like the greats,"* to the relatable, down-to-earth *"Find Your Greatness"* message. Instead of MJ appearing on screen, it was an out-of-shape 12-year-old boy struggling to run down an old country road — but persevering. The message was clear: greatness isn't something unique to a few unicorns (that you can only dream to be like). It's something we're all capable of. Simply put on a pair of Nike trainers, and start your journey.

This resonated with customers so well that Nike saw a $506M increase in revenue and a 55% boost in Nike+ memberships. Social media engagement also soared, with Nike significantly outperforming Adidas in terms of online mentions and new followers[2].

Before you say, "*OK, but that's Nike. We sell B2B software to global enterprises,*" hear me out.

This ad demonstrates a fundamental principle of marketing:

We don't buy products for what they are. We buy better versions of ourselves.

We buy to feel like better parents, better partners, better runners, better people. And we do it in our personal lives and our professional lives.

Let's take me, for example: All my life, I've had this terrible fear of flying. Just the thought of getting on a plane made my heart race, my palms sweat, and my stomach do more backflips than an Olympic gymnast. And yet, skydiving became one of my all-time favorite hobbies. How?

I wanted to impress a crush.

He was a skydiver and I was smitten. I wanted him to see that I was a cool, exciting person. The kind of person who wasn't afraid of anything. So before I knew it, I found myself hanging out of a plane, strapped to a skydiving instructor, and nervously peering over a 14,000 ft drop. And while I do remember thinking, "How the eff did I end up here!?" in hindsight, the answer is obvious.

---

2   https://yourstory.com/2024/07/ike-marketing-strategy-2012-olympics-outsmart-adidas

I was willing to face my biggest fear because I wanted this person to see me in a specific way. Or in more technical terms — I wanted to project a specific social-image. Ultimately, I cared more about how the guy I liked saw me than about the fear that tried to rule me. And these emotions were so powerful that they made me literally jump out of a plane.

Trying to impress your colleagues, your peers and your boss isn't fundamentally different from trying to impress a crush. You want to project a certain image — to be seen in a certain way. To be seen as smart, competent, a good leader, a great colleague, a fantastic addition that deserves that promotion.

All these desires play into the decision-making process for any B2B purchase. We buy to improve performance, to increase the feeling of job security, to be seen as the best problem solver and to influence what those around us think about us. Your customers buy to be the hero that brings in the B2B solution that saves the team five hours a week, or to impress their boss so much they get short-listed for that promotion.

Emotions influence your B2B buyers in so many ways. And the sooner you lean into them, the sooner you'll get your audience off the fence and onto your paid plan.

IT'S ACTUALLY IMPOSSIBLE TO MAKE DECISIONS WITHOUT EMOTION

I *could* spend the next three chapters bombarding you with scientific evidence about the power of emotional targeting — but this is not that kind of book. Instead of getting mired in theory, I want to show you how to use that theory. So, in the spirit of getting to execution quickly, let me tell you about the man who couldn't decide what sandwich he wanted to have for lunch.

'Elliot' was a business man who suffered damage to his ventromedial prefrontal cortex (VMPC) — the part of the brain responsible for processing emotions and emotional regulation. Even though Elliot retained his high intelligence, memory and language skills — helping him think logically about decisions — because he couldn't prioritize his reasoning emotionally, he suffered from severe indecision. Unsurprisingly, this impacted every aspect of his life, right down to what he wanted to eat for lunch.[3]

Elliot's case (he was treated by neuroscientist Antonio Damasio who wrote about his work with brain-injured patients) illustrates that **eliminating emotion takes away a person's power to make confident decisions**. Now consider the effect eliminating emotion from your marketing has on your prospects. Instead of making their lives easy and helping them choose, you've left them with multiple open tabs, trying to objectively compare products with very similar feature sets and promises. Without meaning to, you're trapping them in the depths of analysis paralysis. But they won't stay there long. Unless you give prospects a compelling reason to choose you, they'll be forced to rely on their own gut feel to break the stalemate. This 'fast' thinking is made up of cognitive biases, psychological triggers and preferences that will guide them to a choice.

Everything is designed to make us *think* we're logical
Your mind hungers for certainty. We all want to feel that we've made the best possible choice — that the path we're on is the right one.

---
3   Damasio, A. (1994). Descartes' Error: Emotion, Reason, and the Human Brain. Putnam.

When we ask customers why they chose a specific product, they often focus on the features it has, so naturally, businesses assume showcasing these features will help drive customer certainty and decision-making.

Every feature in a SaaS product is the result of painstaking research, coding, design and testing, so teams want to show them off. With so many features to highlight, it's easy to fall into the trap of making features the centerpiece of your marketing.

But that's not the whole truth. Your customers absolutely look at features — BUT looking at features is not the only thing audiences do when considering a purchase (although it may be the only factor they're consciously aware of). Their decision is also impacted by emotional factors, experiences and cognitive biases that often operate below the surface of awareness.

So you have two options:

You can either leave your customers' gut decision to chance or you can integrate those cognitive biases and triggers into your marketing strategy.

If the second option sounds intriguing, the chapters that follow will show you how to get more strategic than you've ever been before about what to say to your audience so you can optimize for emotion and win more customers.

WHICH EMOTIONS SHOULD YOU OPTIMIZE FOR?

Buying based on how you feel is socially acceptable when you're shopping for something fun and personal. No one is going to judge you for buying a biker jacket because you look like a badass in it. This makes optimizing for emotion in the B2C world easier. If you run a dress shop and ask a customer why they bought a particular dress, most will be happy to tell you the actual reason — their oldest friend is getting married for the third time, they have to go all the way to London for the wedding and they want to look stunning. But if you directly asked a marketing professional why they chose one A/B testing tool over another — and don't dig deeper — they'll probably mumble something about price and features and you'll miss the real reasons. It's no wonder emotion is a blindspot in the B2B space.

To get to the truth, you have to get creative.

 **Emotional targeting case study: Discovering the truth behind customer choices led to nav, homepage and product tour optimization**

A B2B client hired GetUplift to understand what information prospects really needed to understand in order to choose their product over the competition. They'd already surveyed and interviewed customers — but the answers didn't go deep enough.

To get to the truth, we ran hybrid research interviews. We recruited prospects that matched our clients' ICP (ideal customer profile) and were actively shopping for a solution. We then showed them three websites — our client's and two of their top competitors' — and asked them to show us how they'd assess each site to decide if this was a product worth testing.

Because these prospects were actively searching, they naturally fell into their research pattern — and we got to see how prospects actually approached the website when looking for information, where they went and why they did so.

A pattern formed quickly. After glancing at the homepage briefly, the majority navigated to the pricing page to do a quick pricing check and make sure the product was within their price range. Then, they went to the integrations page to check that the solution worked with their current tooling. Next, they went to the feature page and checked that the product had everything on their 'feature shopping list.'

These initial checks were all designed to confirm that the solution in question actually checked the boxes. If it did, prospects started looking for 'emotional confirmation' — they scanned headlines to see if their specific problems were addressed and looked for case studies and testimonials from people with similar job titles. **They were searching for proof that this product was tried, true and effective for their situation.**

After we understood the priority of information, we changed the nav menu to make it easy to get there faster and tested a homepage that prioritized pricing, integrations and features — with copy that addressed specific ICP pains.

But buying decisions aren't just about understanding how prospects look for and prioritize information. You also need to understand which emotions actually drive the purchase.

Emotion often manifests in the concerns and worries your customers have but don't necessarily verbalize. Emotional targeting helps you uncover those silent emotions so you can tap into them as a means to influence buying behavior.

Emotional targeting case study: QA software optimizes for emotions tied to social image

If you really want to optimize website messaging, then you can't just focus your research on how your customers interact with your product — you have to build a clear picture of their entire working life. You have to understand what they do every day — what tasks they prioritize, what meetings they go to and how they tend to structure their days. And then you need to understand how your product fits within that wider context.

When a leading QA solution business approached us at GetUplift because their conversions weren't where they needed to be, we started by building out that context around their ICP — a struggling QA Tester. We ran a series of surveys and interviews designed to help us understand what our ICP did at work and how our client's solution fit within that world.

The research revealed that most QA analysts felt like they were treated like a constant imposition. They were the ones that had to slow launches down so that they could run multiple checks and make sure everything would actually work. And because QA work is essentially 'invisible,' they felt that most of their colleagues didn't understand what they were doing or why it mattered.

Our client's software solved this problem — it gave QA teams the power to showcase all the different tests they ran and made it easy for everyone to see their importance in the process. *(It also made running QA tests easier, of course.)* So instead of focusing on the features, we recommended they focus the copy around what the analyst really wanted — a way to show their colleagues that their job was essential.

SHOW CUSTOMERS YOU UNDERSTAND THEIR PROBLEMS

Google's research shows that prospects are 50% more likely to choose a more expensive product **if they see a personal value in their business purchase decision,** and 8X more likely to pay a premium for basically the same product when they see a personal value is present[4]. In other words, personal value is so powerful that it influences decisions in two distinct ways: first, customers will actively choose a higher-priced product over competitors when they connect with its personal value; and second, even when comparing functionally identical solutions, they're willing to pay significantly more for the one that resonates with them personally. This isn't just about preference — it's about perceived worth transcending price considerations.

---

4   https://www.thinkwithgoogle.com/_qs/documents/1103/promotion-emotion-b2b_articles_3ORqOvz.pdf

After your prospects check that your solution meets their needs for pricing, features, and integrations, they start looking for connection. And once they've checked off everything on their list, they'll lean towards the product that connects with them in a specific way. We've seen it a thousand times over.

To make a decision, your prospects are subconsciously scanning for clues that show you understand their problem and can help them solve it. The more clearly they see their concerns and priorities reflected back at them, the easier it becomes for them to buy from you. Now, let's dig into the framework that will help you do this.

CHAPTER 3

INTRODUCING THE EMOTIONAL TARGETING FRAMEWORK™

SPIDER-MAN HAS SPIDER-SENSE. PROFESSOR X HAS TELEPATHY. MARKETERS HAVE EMOTIONAL TARGETING.

Better results start with understanding your customers. Understanding your customers starts with the Emotional Targeting Framework™

If you want meaningful conversion increases, you have to stop treating your customers like data points, segments and numbers.

Too many coaches, trainers and industry leaders teach B2B marketers to obsess over metrics and data points like age, geographical location, role, browsers and devices—essentially anything they can easily map out on a graph or present in a shiny report. The problem is that when you view your customers like data sheets, you ignore the emotional and social components that drive prospects to buy. Simply put, **you end up selling to the building rather than the people inside it.** This is a problem because it's not the 'building' that makes the decisions, it's your customers. And those customers are driven by fears, desires and deep motivations that go far beyond the broad data points you're used to looking at.

"Sell to people, not buildings" sounds painfully obvious... and yet our behavior doesn't always match up. If you're anything like most smart marketers, as soon as you feel there's a conversion problem you go into Google Analytics. There, you might notice you're getting traffic to the product or pricing page, but too few are converting. GA (and other analytics solutions) helps you point to where the problem lies, which is great. It can even help you identify the customer segments 'failing' to convert. What GA fails to do is help you decide what changes to make to optimize the page. And if you want to meaningfully increase conversions, you need knowledge and insights about what to change and how.

Here's the honest-to-goodness truth: If you've found yourself in this position, it's because you're missing critical information about who your customers are.

Sure, you 'know' them as a 40-55-year-old female in a C-suite position who is most active on Instagram and LinkedIn. But this information doesn't help you figure out what to say in your marketing and how to say it. That's why so many websites skip the 'customer-first' part and stick to talking about the product itself. It's why too many pages end up being a list of features and pricing with a testimonial carousel in there for good measure.

As a result, your audience can't see themselves or their problems and desires reflected on the page, making it difficult for them to choose you and convert.

Imagine if you fed Coca-Cola's demographics and target audience data to ChatGPT and asked it to outline a landing page for you.

ChatGPT

Please outline a landing page for a well-known soda drink.

The details:

- The target audience is adults, children and seniors
- Start with an attention-grabbing headline
- Use the first paragraph to clearly describe what our drink is and its primary benefits
- Use the final section to invite people to buy it

Our main selling points and benefits:

- Just $14.38 for 24 cans
- 140 calories only
- Multiple container options - glass, plastic or can
- You can get multiple sugar free versions!
- Drink has been number one in the world since 1886

 Message ChatGPT

Here's what ChatGPT would tell you to do:

 ChatGPT

- Use a catchy headline such as *"Experience the Classic Refreshment Since 1886"* to immediately capture attention.
- Add a sub-headline: *Refreshing, delicious, and made for everyone*—enjoy the taste that's been delighting people for over a century!
- Use limited-time promotions in your CTA: *Order Now – Get 24 Cans for Just $14.38!*
- Highlight key benefits, like its low calorie count, affordable price and universal appeal.

 Message ChatGPT

This is what the page would look like:

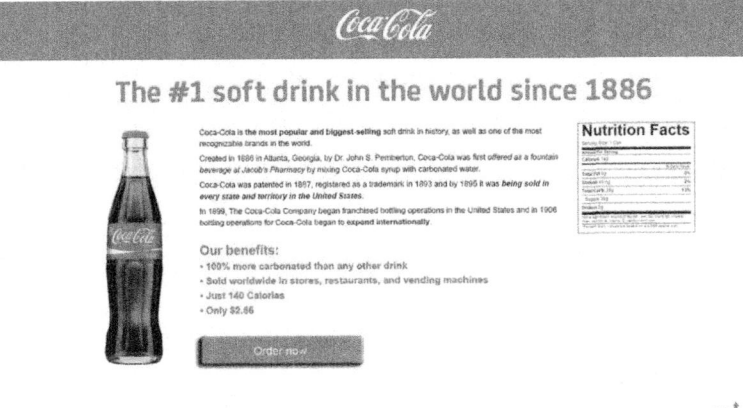

Design credit: Polina Serebrennikova

The idea of Coca-Cola talking to customers like this seems absurd, right? The page could describe just about any other soda. But without realizing it, most B2B brands do the exact same thing—and then wonder why their marketing strategy isn't landing or conversions are falling short.

HOW TO STOP TALKING TO THE BUILDING (AKA YOUR *NEW* APPROACH TO OPTIMIZATION)

If you want to improve your conversions, you need to understand that you are selling to the person behind the screen and not the 'company' (a.k.a. the 'building') in front of you.

This is where the Emotional Targeting Framework will help you stand out. The framework is made up of three foundational pillars (or principles) designed to keep you focused on what matters:

1) Make it all about the customer
2) Don't just say it, help them feel it
3) Run meaningful tests

The pillars are designed to guide everything you do. For the purpose of making this book as actionable as possible, I've divided them up into three steps:

1) Research
2) The emotional targeting audit
3) Testing

You'll use research (Pillar 1) to go beyond data and demographics and uncover what drives your customer's decisions on an emotional level. With that research in hand, you'll then audit your website to see if your messaging, design and customer journey currently speak to the conversion-driving emotions uncovered in your research (Pillar 2). Finally, you'll create hypotheses on what you could change to improve emotional resonance and then set up meaningful tests to validate (Pillar 3).

Applying these pillars will keep you dialed into customer emotions so you can create a more persuasive, high-converting experience—and stop talking to the building once and for all. Once you achieve this shift, you can finally achieve the two fundamental (and commonly neglected) goals of optimization:

Goal #1: To solve your customer's problems
The first and primary goal of optimization is to solve your customer's problems. It's not about whether an animated video or static list of features will increase your conversions by 2%. It's about ensuring

your prospects can see their pains and what they care about on the page so they can immediately connect your product with what it will solve for them.

While the person behind the screen does care about features, they care more about how you can help them solve a specific problem with those features. If you can find the one problem your audience wants to solve, they'll buy from you over your competitors. Take Strata, for example. When they brought us on board to optimize their website, we optimized every page and asset on the site by zooming in on the critical IAM problems Strata's ICPs had and weaving in the connecting thread between them.

Emotional targeting case study: From identity protection to identity hero

Strata hired GetUplift to help optimize their website and campaigns so that they appealed to the right buyers and reflected who they were and what they needed. Strata has excellent Identity Access Management (IAM) expertise and an amazing team devoted to meeting customers' needs. However, the sheer technicality of the product made it difficult for users to understand precisely how Strata could solve their specific problems.

The first step was to conduct exhaustive research. We interviewed and surveyed team members and then conducted an emotional audit of their competitors to understand Strata's existing context. We also conducted UX and heuristic design analysis and voice-of-customer research to know how Strata's customers talk about their identity problems.

Our research led us to identify the missing emotional piece in their messaging around being the identity hero of your company: the hero that reduces tech debt and modernizes non-standard apps without accepting risks.

Previously, Strata's marketing focused solely on features and didn't highlight this unique component that mattered most to its customers. Building this story into its marketing resulted in an increase of **16.3% in overall conversions and a 72.8% increase in Organic search conversions.**

If you want meaningful results like these, you've got to stop talking to 'the building' and focus on solving problems for the person behind the screen.

Goal #2: To make informed decisions
Like most marketers, I used to treat CRO as a tactic aimed at optimizing individual elements to improve certain KPIs. I'd test random stuff like button colors or form fields in the hopes that I'd see an increase in free trial users or sales. Unfortunately, this approach gave me little in the way of results and even fewer ways to scale my insights to other parts of the funnel.

As I wanted to learn more about real optimization (that lasts and has a meaningful effect), I knew I had to uncover how people make decisions. That's when I started exploring emotion and building the framework to connect emotionally with potential customers. My understanding of CRO shifted away from changing elements and towards building a better customer experience focused on understanding and solving customer problems.

Take a traditional A/B test, for example. You test two types of buttons and run with the one that gets more clicks. But this doesn't tell you anything meaningful about your audience. The tests you'll run in Pillar 3will give you knowledge you can use for future experiments to see meaningful uplifts. For example, if you hypothesize that your audience resonates more with pain points around social-image than self-image, it doesn't matter if the new variation is a winner or loser. What matters is that you now have knowledge on what resonates and this can inform your future optimization efforts.

Ultimately, CRO is about understanding who your customer is beyond the 'dry' data and then leveraging those insights to create a customer-FIRST journey or funnel that solves their problems and helps them achieve their goals.

Emotional targeting needs to happen before, during and after you optimize. Until you take the time to understand the emotions that drive customers to buy from you (AKA emotional targeting), you'll be stuck guessing what to change next.

RUN TESTS THAT ACTUALLY GET YOU THE RESULTS THAT YOU NEED

Every test you run should serve a purpose. It should be like a puzzle piece — something that fits within and supports a much bigger picture. It should be meaningful. And **meaningful testing is all about solving people's problems.**

But to solve specific problems, you first need to understand:

1) What your customer's real problem actually is
2) How much of that real problem they expect you to solve
3) Who you're trying to solve the problem for
4) How you're going to test the potential solutions to this problem strategically

If you don't run your optimization program in this way, you won't understand why certain changes produced the outcomes they did. **This makes it challenging to replicate those results and create consistent, predictable growth.**

You see, CRO isn't about metrics. It's not even about conversions. It's about answering critical questions like:

- How do I show prospects the product's clear, real value so they see that this is the right tool for their needs?
- What should the customer journey actually look like? What are the exact steps and paths the ICP needs to take to buy into the offer?
- How do I optimize the product for specific a-ha moments?
- What verticals should we invest in as a business?
- How should we position our pricing and packaging?
- How should we PRICE our products?

All of these questions can and should be answered with your CRO program. But you can only do this when you do customer-first optimization and run meaningful tests.

Let's see how this might play out in real life. For example, during your Emotional Targeting Audit, you may identify that your ideal customers cannot immediately see that your product was built for them. Once you test this hypothesis out on one crucial page on your site (i.e. your homepage), you'll be able to optimize every part of your customer journey, from your ads and landing pages to your pricing, onboarding, packaging and more using this insight.

Running meaningful tests also means you can finally break silos within the organization. It's a common experience for marketing and product or sales teams to struggle to communicate. Marketing sends a bunch of signups or leads, only the sales and/or product team complains that they're not converting. When you run meaningful experiments using this framework, you present your learnings and insights to all teams and come together to say:

> "Hey, this is the problem we're trying to solve. What are you doing about this in the product?"

> "How do you solve this on your sales calls?"

You have the power to bring all teams together to answer critical questions. And the impact that this can have on growth is huge.

WHY THE EMOTIONAL TARGETING FRAMEWORK BELONGS IN YOUR TOOLKIT NOW MORE THAN EVER

It's hard to keep up with new trends in technology. However, there is one thing I know to be true: **technology changes, and humans don't.**

As long as you're selling to humans and not robots, you must make it your priority to understand the people behind the screen. Sure, you can leverage technology to help you do research and analyze your results. We ourselves use a mix of tools to help us execute on the framework. However, even though the tools have changed, the core of what we do hasn't. The focus continues to be on understanding human psychology and why people buy, because the science behind how people make decisions doesn't change. Once you understand this foundational truth, everything else comes into play. You can utilize all the tools and platforms in the world to help you. But first, **you must understand that people don't change.**

The more technical the world becomes, and the more automation and AI come into play, the more you need to do this foundational work of understanding the human psyche and the core of how people make decisions. The world is getting noisier, with everyone competing for attention. When you only focus on technology, you use these tools without the foundation. You're left wondering who the tools are really for.

Ultimately, technology should be another tool you use and not your superpower. **Your superpower should be knowing your customers and understanding the emotions that drive them to buy.** This is what will make you the optimization hero.

We've tested this framework thousands of times, and it's 100% repeatable.

Besides helping our clients increase every metric that counts, the framework has helped so many marketing teams get on the same page, set a clear growth strategy, break silos within their organization

AND create a repeatable, dependable process everyone on the team can follow and use to optimize every single campaign they run.

At first, the shift from best practices to emotional targeting will feel uncomfortable. It will require you to move out of your comfort zone and focus on your customers in a way you've never done before. But when you roll up your sleeves and follow the process, you'll stop guessing what to optimize. You'll have a clear idea of what resonates with your audience, and you'll be able to communicate your process and results to the rest of the team.

This is what gets you recognized in the company as the go-to for having a clear vision and strategy that gets results that warrant celebration.

Once you have the superpower of understanding your audience, you can utilize everything around you to make your product and marketing better. It's skills versus knowledge. Skills can always be taught. You can take a course or sit in front of someone, and they'll teach you how to use AI. But if you're armed with the foundational knowledge of who your customers are, what they feel, and how they want to feel, you'll know what to say to them. And that's exactly what you're going to achieve with Pillar 1.

CHAPTER 4

EMOTIONAL TARGETING™ RESEARCH — WHAT IT IS AND HOW TO RUN IT

BATMAN'S GREATEST WEAPON ISN'T HIS UTILITY BELT; IT'S HIS DETECTIVE SKILLS.

Marketers collect behavioral data like they've gotta catch em' all.

Most of our clients typically have strong demographic information about their customers. On project kick-off calls, we tend to hear a variation of the following:

"Our ICPs are between the ages of 27 and 42. They're based in the US. They belong to one of our three target industries - Healthcare, Manufacturing, and Retail & Consumer Goods. They tend to serve as heads of HR or CTOs. Though we don't want to alienate any CEOs and CFOs reading! Or the team members who'll be using the product. Oh, and our primary ICP is searching for a solution to X but the secondary ICPs need Y and Z."

In other words, our clients have a ton of data. They know what browsers their customers are using, the types of devices they prefer, the side of the world they live in, what their job title is and what pages they visit.

And their product teams are sitting on even more qualitative and quantitative data — they've got research that helps them build product roadmaps and test new pricing strategies. And they know all about features customers like, why they chose one pricing tier over another and how to talk about the solution itself.

What's missing is a way to connect all of that data to the emotional drivers behind decision making — and then apply those insights to different parts of the funnel. Because when you're trying to create a customer journey that resonates on an emotional level, one that captures a prospect's attention and stops them from tab-hopping to your competitor, you need very specific research.

You need the kind of research that uncovers the ins and outs of who your customers are and what motivated them

In the words of a wonderful client, while they shared a gorgeous Notion project board with enough customer information to make the most dedicated of researchers happy, *"We have so much data on our customers, it's hard to know what to prioritize and how to apply it properly to our customer journey."*

Too many teams find themselves in this exact pickle. You have so much knowledge available that it's really hard to know what to *actually* do next.

Emotional Targeting™ research solves this problem. Instead of giving you more information, it focuses on answering key strategic questions that help you turn 'information' into practical insights. It tells you WHY people buy from you, what frustrates them on a daily basis, what they're worried about and how they're hoping to feel after finding a solution.

If you can, I recommend making one person on your team responsible for creating and analyzing surveys rather than assigning all research to one person. The more you can diversify your research, the more you can avoid bias. If you do it all on your own, you're more likely to cling to one cool insight you found and then look for it throughout the research process.

By the time you've completed it, you'll know exactly what to do next. In this chapter, we're going to walk through the type of research we usually run, why we run it and what makes it different from what you have on hand.

RESEARCH METHOD #1: CUSTOMER-FOCUSED SURVEYS

A customer-focused survey is the gift that will keep on giving — long after you collect and analyze the answers. It will help you understand:

- What drives customers to stop doing what they're doing and start searching for a new solution
- How they find you
- What made them decide to go deeper into your product and learn about you
- Why they ultimately chose you

The two types of Emotional Targeting™ surveys
To get a fuller picture of what's driving customers to buy from you, there are two types of surveys I recommend you use — visitor surveys and customer surveys.

Visitor surveys
Visitor surveys are surveys that trigger when a person first arrives on a high-traffic or high-value landing page. (Visually, they're very similar to the 2-3 question 'chat-style' pop-ups that show up on websites asking about your experience.)

The purpose of visitor surveys is to uncover what brought users to a specific part of your website in the first place. They help you pinpoint the top pains visitors are experiencing with their current solution so you can understand what's driving them to look for a product like yours. They help identify:

- The hesitations and concerns preventing visitors from converting

- The information they're looking for that will convince them to give your solution a try

From a technical perspective, visitor surveys should usually show up when people first land on a specific page. They should be used strategically based on where the conversion happens — use a tool like Google Analytics to identify where your best customers are converting (e.g., your pricing page), and then place the survey there.

The responses from your visitor surveys will then inform the questions you ask in your customer interviews — but we'll talk more about that later.

Customer surveys

Customer surveys are surveys that go to the specific customer segments you're trying to learn more about.

The purpose of this type of survey is to help you learn more about a specific customer type so that you can answer strategic questions about their journey. We typically run these surveys by:

- Emailing a customer segment and asking them to take a quick survey
- Embedding a survey on a 'thank you' page
- Showing the survey in the product dashboard after the customer takes a specific action

The segment you survey depends on your goals, but we tend to focus on segments like:

- Customers who purchased between three and nine months ago and log into the solution at least once a week *(great for seeing how active new customers are using the product)*
- Customers who purchased less than three months ago and log in 3+ times a week *(great for seeing how new users adopt and explore the product and identifying key wins and frustrations)*
- Customers who renewed within the last month and remain active users *(great for seeing what keeps people using your solution and for identifying any frustrations around re-purchasing)*

Your survey placement should be determined by your research goals. That way, you can get the responses you need to understand why customers choose your solution and the emotions that drive that choice. The CEO who is desperate to solve a pain is fundamentally different from the customer who has been using your product for 6months and is seeing amazing results.

Thank you page surveys are great if your goal is to understand the lead up to purchase. Because customers have just bought, their pains, desires and hesitations are fresh in their mind. Their answers are likely to be more accurate than six months down the line, when they've probably forgotten what was going on in their mind the day they converted. If you want fresh voice-of-customer data on what was going on at the moment of conversion, you need to ask at the moment of conversion.

In-product surveys can help you understand customer emotions around specific a-ha moments. For example, the a-ha moment for Bitly — one of our clients — comes after a person has created a certain number of QR codes or links. Bitly knows they want more of these types of customers using their product, so it was logical to send a survey once a customer reached this moment.

Email surveys help you reach a wider net of customers by showing up in their inbox. You can highly segment who you're sending these out to and automate them so they continue collecting data on an ongoing basis. Since you will need a survey tool, you can use it to segment your surveys and run longer ones that are personalized and change based on their responses.

The valuable information you gain through surveys

Customer-first surveys help you gain a deeper understanding of your customers' minds and emotions (unlike product-first surveys that miss crucial context). The right questions reveal what pain your product solves for them so you can uncover the real value you bring to customers. By comparing these two approaches side-by-side, you'll see why customer-first questions generate much more valuable insights:

Product-first survey questions: <typically multiple choice>	Customer-first survey questions: <typically open ended>
Why do you like this feature?	What's the #1 problem <solution> eliminates or lessens for you?
Why did you choose this pricing tier?	What made you feel confident <pricing tier> was the right option for your team?
What do you think of the new website?	How would you describe <solution> to a friend or colleague in the same field as you?

What almost stopped you from converting?	Think back to before the trial — when did you realize you needed a solution like <name>?
Why did you choose <solution>?	What made you confident <solution> could eliminate or lessen <mentioned pain> for you?

Focusing questions around the customer and keeping them open-ended makes a huge difference in response quality. Just compare the product-first responses our client initially received to the valuable insights they gained from our customer-first survey approach:

Product-first survey responses:	Customer-first survey responses:
Easy to use	"Important tasks keep getting buried in long email threads and it's frustrating trying to figure out what needs attention and what is just noise."
It's within the budget	"It's really important to us that we have unlimited messaging history so new hires can find old threads easily. But we also have a relatively small team right now. So the Pro plan felt like the right fit."
It's easy to navigate	"It makes communication so easy. You'll save yourself hours because you're not having to hop on unnecessary meetings or comb through old email threads."
Price	"So it was actually pretty urgent because we upset a major client after three team members promised entirely different things. It was really embarrassing and honestly, we're lucky they didn't walk. We couldn't afford something like this ever happening again."

Needed a solution that fit into the budget	"I think it was the fact there were channels for every project. We juggle a lot of projects at once so that was good. Also, we saw other small marketing teams were using it so that made it easier to convince my boss."

Take the responses above, for example. There are several key emotional triggers including the embarrassment of upsetting a client because the team was disorganized. Or the search for certain social proof they knew their boss would likely feel good about.

Understanding how many responses you need

At a minimum, you want to collect at least 50 quality responses before you pause the survey. The sweet spot tends to be between 150 and 300 responses — this gives you enough information to start seeing patterns emerging without tying your team up for days reviewing answers.

How to avoid 'over-surveying' and irritating your customers

Before we move on to the next research method, I want to address the elephant in the room. You're scared that by asking your customers' questions, you'll annoy them so much that they'll abandon your product and your email list while they're at it. Conducting emotional targeting research for hundreds of brands has shown me that the opposite is true.

Not only are you not annoying your customers, but you're showing them you care about their opinions and needs. You aren't a brand that only cares about doing what everyone else is doing. You care about solving your customers' problems - which is ultimately what optimization is all about.

But to avoid the risk, make sure that any surveys you send are as concise as possible, easy to fill out and only go out to specific customer segments.

RESEARCH METHOD #2: MEANINGFUL CUSTOMER INTERVIEWS

Customer interviews help you go deeper and uncover the words, sentiments and tone customers use when describing their pains or a solution. They help you dig into the themes uncovered by the surveys — and deliver a great foundation for testimonials, customer stories and future copy.

Emotional Targeting Case Study: How Upright embraced the embarrassing emotion standing in the way of conversions

Upright - a brilliant brand that helps people permanently eliminate back pain and fix their posture has a near perfect product. (I should know, I've tested it!). Every time you slouch, Upright's trainer — a small device placed on your back — vibrates and reminds you to sit up straight based on biofeedback. It's simple and super effective. And it's one of the few products that could justifiably be sold to 'everyone'.

Due to its universality, Upright's approach on their website messaging and funnel had always been the same: they described the product, listed the features and showed the science. But while the product delivered on its promise, new prospects had trouble believing that a device this small could actually make a difference. Something in the messaging was missing the mark and they asked GetUplift to help.

Our Emotional Targeting research uncovered that Upright's best customers were people who spent a lot of time sitting at their desks. This level of sedentary behavior led to back problems and frustration with their poor posture. But changing was proving difficult — as Upright's ICPs sat in front of their computers, hard at work, they'd forget to sit back. And every evening, they paid the price for that poor posture and swore that the next day, they'd remember to make it a priority. And so the cycle would start again. Digging deeper into their stories revealed that people felt guilty about forgetting to prioritize their posture and powerless to do anything about it.

So — instead of avoiding the guilt — we brought it into the messaging. The new copy addressed the guilt directly and assured prospects that their poor posture was not their fault. We highlighted the 700,000 customers who were just like them — suffering in silence until they chose to 'outsource' the responsibility for reminding them to sit properly to Upright. Seeing their deepest issues addressed on the page resonated deeply and resulted in 33.69% uplift in transactions and 25% increase in revenue.

Choosing the right customers to interview
When planning research interviews, focus on the best-fit customers you want more of. Interview customers that use the product in a successful way (depending on how you measure engagement) and

became customers less than six months ago. *(These customers are more likely to be able to recall those feelings and insights easily.)*

The customers who answer your survey are likely to also agree to an interview, which is why we like to include a question in our surveys asking if they'd be up to it. You'd be surprised how many people agree.

What to ask customers during an Emotional Targeting interview
Use interviews to further uncover the top pains that led customers to you, the top desired outcomes you're hoping for and to decode how they make purchasing decisions. The trick with interviews is to keep digging until you get to the core of the answer — don't take customers at their 'surface level' word.

Here's an example for a recent client we worked with:

- **We asked:** What was going on in your life that made you search for a solution like <brand>?
- **The go-to response:** "I was searching for a better way to do <X>"
- **So we followed up:** What made you search for a better way to do <X>?
- **The answer:** "We kept missing client tickets and emails and we were getting duplicate messages... sometimes we'd reply twice, it was messy and the team was frustrated"

A deeper, more specific answer that described how they felt before hiring our clients software to help them.

Here's another example:

- **We asked:** So what's your favorite thing about using <brand> now?
- **Answer:** "We finally have one place to do it all" *(cue the all time favorite B2B headline!)*
- **Follow up:** What made that your favorite thing?
- **Answer**: "We used to reply to the customer from multiple channels, with different names and we wasted time on these. Once we even lost a client because of this! Now we don't have to login to multiple tools each time anymore, and the team can continue previous conversations seamlessly instead of starting a new thread each time and confusing our customers."

The 'follow up' answer gives more meaningful and deep reasoning to why an all-in-one platform matters to their ICP and can help the team optimize how they speak about their all-in-one platform.

The deeper you dig into the reasons prospects give you, the more people will share insightful stories about what nudged them to buy. You'll hear from the technophobe who was worried they wouldn't be able to pull off the transition until Gemma from CS got on a call with them and spent 20 minutes walking them through how it all works. In the space of two minutes, you'll have a new testimonial AND important information about your ICP so you can address their concerns and pair them with powerful social proof.

Running great interviews

Great interviews are about going beyond and creating a space for customers to just talk. As tempting as it is, you must resist the urge to give feedback on customer answers. This will help you avoid creating a conversation around one specific thing instead of going deeper. 90% of the time you should be nodding your head and asking why.

Throughout the interview, pay attention to how customers describe the different pains they've had in the past and the problems that were solved for them. Notice their tone and voice when they describe your product and how it solved their problems. Pay attention to pauses and excitement when talking about specific features.

How many interviews should you do?
In an ideal world, you want to interview at least ten people from one specific ICP to go deeper into the pains, outcomes and concerns that you uncovered during the survey stage. However, quality is better than quantity here. Five interviews where you go deep into the pains of your ICP are worth 10X more than 100 surface-level interviews.

If you have more than one ICP, speak to at least five in each category *(though ideally it would be a minimum of 10)*. What you might find is that even though you have three distinct personas or jobs to be done, they all have very similar emotional drivers.

RESEARCH METHOD #3: USING SOCIAL LISTENING TO FILL THE GAPS

'Social listening' helps you collect the specific language your audience uses to describe their pains and frustrations when you're not actively watching them.

It allows you to 'drop in' on the conversations your ICP is having around products like yours. This can help you fill in any information gaps.

What is social listening?
Social listening is monitoring what people are saying about their challenges and the solutions they've tried in your space.

One great method, called review mining, involves going into reviews for books that are trying to solve the same problems you're solving. If you have accounting software, read "Accounting for Dummies." Go to Amazon and look at the reviews. Ask yourself: what are people complaining about? What are they missing? What's the number one thing everyone says sucks about the book? If people are complaining, it means they care, which means you should pay attention to it.

If you're an e-commerce brand, look at the reviews your competitors are getting. If you're a B2B company, look at G2Crowd, and the other spaces where people are commenting about your product or similar products. All this will help you get to know your ICP better.

People use sites like Reddit to do product research, compare solutions, and ask questions because *"the answers feel more authentic."* Reddit, LinkedIn, Quora and Facebook are filled with conversations and emotionally-charged voice-of-customer research you should be reading and listening to. Social groups are also a great place to fish out the people who would be valuable to interview so you can go deeper without contacting a single customer.

What should I be looking for?
Just like in the survey and interview phase, you're looking for pains, desired outcomes and hesitations people experience before investing in solutions like yours. Look for the 'keyboard ragers' and the complainers and for the helpful people describing their experiences in great detail.

You should also look for opportunities where you can stand out. I can't tell you the number of times my team has looked at hundreds of reviews for our client's competitors and identified one thing everyone is complaining about. We've then used this as a distinct opportunity to position our clients against the competition.

For example, when we do comparison pages, we use the thing everyone's complaining about as the crosshead, e.g., 'no constant upsells.' It's a great way to get language from the people who are buying from your competitors when they should buy from you.

RESEARCH METHOD #4: EMOTIONAL COMPETITOR ANALYSIS

The difference between a regular competitor analysis vs. an emotional competitor analysis boils down to what you're looking for.

When conducting traditional competitor research, the new norm is to use AI to drum up a comparative table of features, pricing and technical aspects like integrations. What you don't include is who your competitors are speaking to, the problem they're trying to solve or the value proposition. Without this information, you're unable to understand where the market is emotionally or how your product fits in.

This is where emotional competitor analysis comes in. The aim isn't to achieve the competitive edge by dropping your pricing to match your cheapest competitor. It's to position yourself as the obvious choice based on the emotional needs your competitors aren't addressing.

What you should be analyzing
When conducting a competitor analysis, most companies look at pricing, features, technology and other product-related info. They'll look at net worth, the team size and an overview of what the company is.

But to understand the behavioral triggers that drive the purchase, you need to look at their marketing strategy and how they resonate with other people — a.k.a. the people who should be buying from you but are instead buying from your competitor. What we're interested in is their messaging, their offer and the audience they're speaking to.

Questions to ask yourself when conducting emotional competitor analysis:

- Who is this competitor speaking to? Are they trying to capture a broad audience or are they focusing on a specific ICP(s)?
- What is their main promise to the audience?
- What emotional outcomes are they highlighting?
- What are some of the repeating words they're using in their copy and messaging?
- Are they using real images or animations?
- What social proof are they using?
- What stories are they telling?

What's the purpose of my emotional competitor analysis?

The purpose of your emotional competitor analysis is to understand:

1) what everyone else is saying
2) what they *aren't* saying

When you understand these two things, you will start to see opportunities to stand out from the noise. For example, let's say you're tasked with selling an AI writing tool. You notice that all your competitors are talking about speed and how fast you can bust out content. However, while your tool is fast, it also takes a unique approach to integrating brand voice. When you look back at the data you collected during social mining, you notice lots of your competitors' customers are complaining about the output being too generic. Your customers don't have that issue with your tool. Now you have an opportunity to differentiate yourself.

When to conduct emotional competitor analysis

You should conduct your emotional competitor analysis AFTER you do your customer surveys and interviews. By this point, you should have a better understanding of the pains and desires that drive customers to purchase. This means when analyzing what your competitors are doing, you should be able to see whether they're talking about these pains and desires or ignoring them, like in the example above.

How many competitors should I be looking at?

We usually recommend looking at all of your primary competitors. But if you want to go above and beyond, you should also look at two to three indirect competitors — brands who solve the same emotional problem for customers but do so with a different feature set.

For example, if you're selling a creative design tool, it's easy to pull up a list of competitors like Canva or Adobe. However, your prospects might also be considering solutions that aren't SaaS tools, like hiring a freelancer on Fiverr or training someone on their team to get better at Google Slides. Your emotional competitor analysis then reveals that hiring on Fiverr is causing a lot of pain among the team because they don't have the budget for a full-stack designer and the freelancers they hire rarely understand the brief. Now you can position your product as the path of least resistance because it's easier than Google Slides and faster than chasing freelancers.

PREPARING TO SYNTHESIZE

Once you or your team have completed the recommended research in this chapter, you should have a diverse mix of assets, including:

- 100-150 survey responses
- 5-10 interview transcripts
- 50 snippets from your social listening
- Emotional competitor analysis of 5 to 10 other companies

Now, let's go into how to turn this information into valuable, usable insights so you can get closer to breaking the deadly hamster wheel of optimization once and for all.

CHAPTER 5

SYNTHESIZING YOUR RESEARCH

PROFESSOR X'S POWER ISN'T MIND-READING — IT'S UNDERSTANDING WHAT PEOPLE WON'T SAY OUT LOUD.

After completing the research phase, it's time to organize it. The goal here is to connect the dots between the customer emotions and motivations you uncovered. This means looking beyond isolated responses and **uncovering the patterns, themes and underlying desires that shape how your audience makes decisions** — and then pulling these into a Customer Compass *(more about that at the end of the chapter)*.

No matter what you're selling, prospects are almost always going to be asking themselves these two questions:

1) How am I going to feel about myself after purchasing?
2) How are other people going to feel about me?

Whether they're asking these questions consciously or subconsciously, they are asking them. You see, a lot of responsibility is involved in choosing a tool for the company. Your customer's decision is tied to two critical driving forces — self-image and social image.

The two critical driving forces in decision making	
Self-image	Social-image
Your 'self-image' is how you want to feel about yourself. Your customer's self-image is linked to how they want to feel about themselves after they research, choose, purchase and onboard a new solution.	Your 'social-image' is how you want other people to see you. Your customer's social-image is linked to how they want their colleagues, managers and company leaders to see them during the research, selection, purchasing and implementation process.

And your job is to identify all of the emotions associated with your ICP's self-image and social-image.

Self-image	Social-image
Feeling like they're progressing in their career	Getting a promotion because they picked the tool that had a massive impact on team productivity
Trusting themselves more with bigger decisions	Getting a mention in an executive meeting because they performed outstandingly and getting that recognition feels amazing
Feeling valuable to the company and not like an imposter	No more sitting there with their camera off on Zoom meetings because everyone knows they have nothing to contribute
Feeling more confident in their work	Concerns about the embarrassment of getting a tool that people won't use
Forgiving themselves for the bad job they did on PPC ads 3 years ago	Worry that important information might get deleted in the changeover and they'll look bad in front of the whole team

How to pull these emotions out of your research

To help yourself spot patterns in your research, look for any instances where your audience mentions other people: their colleagues' faults (or successes), or their interactions with other people. These are clear indicators your prospect is concerned about social image. When you're going through surveys or interviews, if you hear the respondent talk about other people, make a note. Highlight it in green so you can come back to it later.

When they talk about how they feel or how they want to feel, highlight it in pink. This is self-image. When you go back through your data to look for top pain points and desired outcomes, you'll be able to quickly and easily organize them into social and self-image buckets (i.e., the emotions that drive conversions). If your sheet is looking more like Shrek than Barbie, this is a potential indicator that your audience is more motivated by social-image than self-image when purchasing solutions like yours.

Self-image	Social-image
"I was at a stage where I wanted to feel like I'm moving forward in my career, like I'm actually growing and not stuck."	"I wanted to pick something that makes a big difference. Like, something that gets me noticed for a promotion."
"Sometimes I doubt myself when I'm making big decisions, and I want to feel like I can trust myself."	"It feels amazing when someone calls out my work in a meeting — like, it's nice to be recognized."
"There are times I feel like I don't belong, like I'm not really valuable, and I really wanted to shake that."	"I hate sitting in Zoom meetings with my camera off because I don't have anything valuable to add."
"I wish I could just feel more confident about the work I'm doing. I'm always second-guessing."	"I'd be really embarrassed if I pushed for a tool and then no one on the team actually used it."
"I still beat myself up over a bad campaign I ran years ago. I wanted to let that go and move forward."	"I'm scared of something going wrong in the changeover and it making me look bad in front of everyone."

It can be easy to get lost in the raw data as you're reflecting on your research. Organizing the data into these buckets will help you be decisive about what data to ignore and what to pay attention to. As you're doing this, you might start to form a hypothesis about how people feel about themselves and how they want to feel (self-image). Then, you might form a hypothesis about what they think other people think of them and how they want people to think of them (social-image).

Look for repeatable phrases and recurring themes — zoom out and look at the big picture. Identify the key themes that come up in the majority of responses.

Answering the call to go deeper
One of the challenges with emotional targeting is that emotions tend to be complex. It's rare that one emotion alone will drive purchasing behavior and even rarer that respondents will tell you what they're feeling in detail. Often, this is simply because your customers aren't consciously aware of the emotions that drove them to buy.

So what do you do? Asking yourself the right questions can help you read between the lines and translate what people say into what they actually mean.

Here are some quick-hitters:

1) What is really at stake for this person if they don't solve this problem?
2) How do they want to feel once they solve it?
3) What are they worried will happen if they make the wrong call?

Answering these questions off the bat is challenging, but the richer your research is, the easier it becomes to decipher what customers really mean when they say certain things (and test them).

For example:

What they say	What they really mean
"I don't think this has the features we need."	...What if this doesn't solve the problem and I get blamed for picking the wrong tool?
"I'm not sure my manager will approve."	...I'm not sure I have enough information about this tool to properly sell it to my boss and they don't trust me enough to choose this product unless I know absolutely everything.
"It seems a little too expensive for us right now."	...What if I convince my boss to invest, it doesn't deliver and I look irresponsible?
"I need to check with my boss before moving forward."	...I don't want to take the blame if this goes wrong — it needs to be someone else's call.
"It's not a priority right now."	...I'm not confident this will really add enough value to be worth pushing for.

We can't know for sure exactly what will drive more prospects to buy from you without testing. You might suspect that prospects aren't buying because they're worried they will look bad if the tool doesn't deliver, but it's only when you test that messaging on the page that you'll know if it resonates or not. If it does, great. If it doesn't, you've learned something about your customer. And that's valuable too.

USING YOUR MESSAGING INSIGHTS TO BUILD A CUSTOMER COMPASS

The goal of Emotional Targeting™ research is to create a Customer Compass — a high-level, strategic slide deck that guides your optimization efforts.

This Compass is a detailed profile of who your customer is, emotionally and psychologically. It captures your ICP's true intent, needs and the roadblocks that prevent them from converting.

You'll use it to get your team and any future hires or subcontractors on the same page. **Your Customer Compass will help you identify the words, design and overall customer journey you'll use for successful optimization.** It should essentially bridge the gap between 'what people are saying' and 'what we should optimize on our home page.' Every company should have this in their arsenal.

Your Customer-first Compass should show:

- Who you are, who you serve, and what you do for them
- The main pain points and desires your customers face and the emotions around each one *(with real world customer quotes to support each pain and desire)*
- A summary of the core emotions customers feel while searching for a solution
- A summary of the core emotions customers want to feel after finding the right solution
- The #1 roadblock (pushback, concern, hesitation) that prevents people from converting with you

- What these objections could mean subconsciously
- The #1 thing people need to read/see and feel in order to convert
- Summary of your competitor's strengths, weaknesses and your opportunity to stand out
- Words your customers use to describe you

Curious what your Customer Compass should look like?

Scan the QR code to get a sample of the slide deck we use for our clients PLUS access the complete companion workbook to this book.

If your brand has more than one customer type, you should complete the customer-focused slides for each of them. You should be able to list the top three pains, desires and hesitations for each. But remember, you don't want to overwhelm the rest of your team with research. You want this to become a must-read deck that clearly outlines who your customers are and why they buy from you.

COMING FULL CIRCLE: YOUR CUSTOMER COMPASS SHOULD INFORM YOUR RESEARCH

The end goal of your research is to create a complete Customer Compass. But, in order to run effective research, you should always confirm the goals of your Compass before putting a single survey question on paper. All great research starts with a strong hypothesis — you need to understand exactly what your end goal is so that you can get the information you need like:

- The specific pains and challenges your prospects deal with before finding a solution
- Desired outcomes your customers want to achieve
- Concerns and hesitations your audience have before converting

Each of these categories focuses on your customer and not your product. Framing your research in this way will gear it towards finding the messages that will emotionally resonate with your audience.

The 5 reflective questions to guide your research:

1) What are some of the repeating phrases, words or adjectives people use to describe the challenges they had before?
2) What are some of the repeating phrases, words or adjectives people use to describe the outcomes they got?

EMOTIONAL TARGETING

3) What are some of the repeating phrases, words or adjectives people use to describe what makes your solution different?
4) What are some of the repeating phrases, words or adjectives people use to describe what they don't like about other solutions?
5) What makes your solution uniquely qualified to solve these specific challenges (#1) and deliver those outcomes (#2)?

The five reflective questions will solve the problem of how to synthesize your research. More crucially, they will help you maintain a focus on what you're ultimately looking for when executing the research phase. This will help you get more strategic about what you ask your customers, so the answers you collect make optimization 10X smoother.

CHAPTER 6

RUNNING AN EMOTIONAL TARGETING™ AUDIT

LIKE DOCTOR STRANGE DISCOVERING HIDDEN DIMENSIONS, THIS AUDIT REVEALS WHAT'S REALLY AFFECTING YOUR CONVERSIONS.

After you get to know your customers on a deeper level, it's time to put that information to use and run an emotional targeting audit.

In this audit, you'll ask yourself a set of critical questions to determine how each piece of your customer journey works together to move prospects toward action. You'll be looking at the way color, design, strategic layout and messaging interact on the page and then identify areas for improvement.

This emotional targeting audit is not about going into your website and reviewing it through a best practice lens. You'll examine what you're doing and ask yourself if you're addressing the key insights that you've uncovered in your most critical pages and funnel steps, and then create a roadmap of what you're going to test and change. You'll look at your funnel holistically and determine if it all works together.

Are you telling one coherent story from the search term (or from the ad people click) all the way through to your onboarding emails? In short, this serves a higher strategic purpose — it's a way to take all of the messaging and emotional insights you uncovered and use them to evaluate what's working and what isn't. **This sets you up to create strong hypotheses and run meaningful tests that create growth beyond arbitrary metrics.**

WHAT IS AN EMOTIONAL TARGETING AUDIT?

No amount of tweaking buttons, headlines and images will get the results you need — but this audit will. It will help you understand why people aren't converting *and* it'll answer the long standing question: what the F should I change? Here, you'll uncover why people aren't converting, easily find the gaps and missing pieces in your strategy and stop wasting hours trying to figure out what's wrong with your marketing.

While the steps in this chapter are focused on page-by-page audits, you can use this approach everywhere you're speaking with customers—your entire website, emails, navigation, ads, and more. This allows you to zoom out to the bigger picture, identify if you're speaking to your ICP in ways that truly resonate and fix your overarching messaging for company-wide growth.

To conduct your audit, you'll answer a series of critical questions designed to help you identify opportunities to improve conversions. You'll review the copy, colors, visuals and the design. Everything on the page and throughout your customer journey needs to support your message and the problem you're solving.

These questions focus on emotional targeting. Your answer to each will either be a yes or a no. Once you've identified which answers are a no, you can come up with a hypothesis on how to optimize to make it a yes. This increases the effectiveness of any test you run — instead of guessing and hoping for the best, you're diagnosing a problem and trying to fix it.

HOW TO AUDIT YOUR CUSTOMER JOURNEY

Before we get to the 'how,' a quick caveat: the emotional targeting audit should come after you've fixed 'the basics.' Of course, you need to look at user recordings and do a heuristic analysis to make sure your website is performing to the best UX principles. You already know you need to check if your buttons actually work, that you have the same color on every button and that your website follows a set color scheme.

Let's say you're tasked with driving more free trials to your product. You go into Google Analytics and spot the leak. Conversions are dropping off on your pricing page. Now, you need to decide what changes to make to increase conversions, so you ask yourself the reflective questions. Because you have emotional targeting research, it should be immediately clear what you're doing wrong.

Below, we'll run through each of the reflective questions and explore how to think about each, so you can confidently answer yes or no.

Q1: Can my prospects see their pains reflected in every step of the journey? (i.e. Are you establishing trust from the get go and proving you know them? Or does your customer journey lean heavily into the generic themes they're used to seeing?)

To answer this question, you'll look to see if your copy, imagery and user experience are addressing the top three pain points you identified in the research phase. If you're simply talking about your features, technology and pricing without connecting it to your prospect's current pains, your potential customers won't see themselves on the page.

For example, when the membership site iPhone Life hired us to optimize their customer journey, we identified that their existing messaging focused on those in their fifties (plus or minus) wanting to learn more about their Apple devices and how to use them. Our research revealed that the real motivator was that customers felt embarrassed and tired of having to ask their kids and grandkids how to use their phones. They wanted to feel self sufficing and smart — to do things their friends couldn't without any help. When we optimized the sales page to reflect these pains, readers felt seen. As a result, iPhone Life saw an 18% uplift in sales.

Q2: Can my customers immediately (and clearly) see what's in it for them on this page?

Your customer research showed you what customers care about. It gave you information about how people feel right now and how they want to feel after finding a solution.

If you're not solving the appropriate customer problem on every single page, they won't take the next step in the funnel. People are bouncing from solution to solution, hoping to find 'the right one.' If they don't immediately see how you solve their particular problem in your ads, emails and pages, they're out of there.

With this in mind, every single page you create, campaign you launch and email you send should immediately convey the problem you're solving and the emotional outcome your solution will provide them. You have to highlight the features you have and marry them with the outcomes your customer wants and cares about in the particular step of the customer journey that they're in. The images you use should support that story — they should help the customer connect to the problem emotionally and feel seen.

Q3: Am I using the actual words my customers and prospects use to describe their pains or challenges?

High-converting copy is like a perfect mirror — it reflects customers' feelings back to them. It should be built using the words your customers and prospects use to describe their pains and challenges so they can understand how your solution fits into the context of their lives.

If the copy was written pre-research, you have an opportunity to optimize your website using language from the quotes you collected in the research phase. Use your fresh messaging insights to check if your current messaging matches the emotions you identified and then create tests to pit against the control.

Like we did for one of our clients when we optimized their paid landing pages to reflect the biggest frustrations we uncovered: spending endless hours designing an outstanding presentation. Our research revealed that designers felt stressed and overwhelmed creating these presentations. With so many software options available, what resonated most wasn't just another tool, it was the promise of creating presentations faster WHILE standing out in the sea of similar slide decks everyone was producing. We mirrored this specific pain point in their landing page copy.

Q4: Do your design, UX, colors and images all support and PROVE your main message? (Is every single element in your funnel designed to drive the message home and help prospects feel seen?)

Now that you have your research, you'll be able to see whether the pains, desires and hesitations you identified in the research phase are present on the page. If these are missing, your customers won't feel seen. If you're talking about features without marrying each to a pain or desired outcome, you're probably not connecting with your customers in a way that impacts conversions. If all the images are of your product and your testimonials are raving indiscriminately about your technology, you're not addressing what matters to the people you're selling to.

Q5: Am I using stories that resonate?

Now that you know what customers care about, you'll be able to see if you're telling stories that resonate.

Every story should reflect the customer's challenges and wants back to them. They should show people in similar situations — with job titles and accolades your ICP can identify with — overcoming frustrations using your product. Because stories are simply about how great your product is, they're highly unlikely to resonate.

Q6: Am I highlighting the outcomes customers care about or am I just speaking about the features and how the solution works?

You should spend twice as much talking about what your product does for your customers as you do talking about the features and how your solution works. Every feature should be paired with an outcome that your customers have told you they care about.

The table below shows a before vs. after headline for one of our clients, PowerUp Toys. See how the 'before' describes what the product is while the 'after' connects the product to the outcome customers want? We paired the new headline with a photo of a grandfather and grandson flying the plane together. The new changes helped us increase PowerUp Toys sales by 95%.

The question is, does your headline look more like the before or the after?

BEFORE Emotional Targeting	AFTER Emotional Targeting
SMARTPHONE CONTROLLED PAPER AIRPLANE	For flight-lovers, problem-solvers, tinkerers, inventors and RC hobbyists eager to take on a unique challenge... FOLD A PAPER PLANE. ADD POWERUP. CONTROL IT WITH YOUR PHONE. Explore the limits of aerodynamics by creating unique planes that push your creativity — and our propeller — to the limit. Or use one of our pre-designed models to start flying with friends in minutes.

Q7: Can a prospect immediately see WHAT action they need to take on the page to get the promised emotional outcome?

Customers should be clear what will happen when they click on a button. If your customers are confused while trying to navigate your site, your conversions will drop.

If your buttons and menu items don't clearly state the emotional outcome prospects will get when they click, this is a potential (and unexpected) opportunity for optimization.

Q8: Am I using relevant social proof that directly dismantles my ICP's top three concerns/hesitations? Or is my social proof generic?

When you audit through a best practice lens, you can give yourself a pat on the back because you've included logos and testimonials that say you're amazing. **But that's not what social proof is actually for.**

You should use social proof to solve the objections and emotional concerns your prospects have. If your testimonials only focus on how great your solution is and aren't strategically placed to help customers overcome specific hurdles, you're missing a key optimization opportunity. Effective social proof should directly address the specific objections stopping prospects from converting. For example, if customers share that they're concerned about the transition from their current software, share a testimonial from someone raving about how seamless the changeover was. Remember — prospects will believe customers like them more than they'll believe claims that you make.

Q9: Does the page use easy-to-follow design cues? (Is the use of color in CTAs and highlighted elements consistent?)

There are many types of readers, including those who will read every word and those who will skim. You should optimize your page so skim readers can find the information they care about quickly. For example, every time they see a pink element, they know it's a headline they need to read. When they see tabs, they know they can dig deeper to get more info if they need it. And when they see a blue background, for example, they know it's a testimonial. In comparison, most designers just highlight what they think needs highlighting from a 'what looks good' perspective. All sorts of pieces get put in huge fonts or animated with no strategy behind them. If your page is filled with flashing fonts and random fonts and colors, the page you're auditing doesn't use easy-to-follow design cues.

* * *

There you have it. A list of nine questions to ask yourself any time you audit a page on your website, ad, landing page—any step in your customer journey.

Emotional Targeting Audit Questions:

- Can my customers see their pains reflected on this page? (i.e. is it focused on their problems or does it focus on the product too heavily without relating it to the customer's needs?)
- Can my customers immediately (and clearly) see what's in it for them on this page?
- Am I using the words my customers and prospects use to describe their pains or challenges?
- Will my customers feel seen when they read this page? (Am I addressing what matters to them?)
- Am I using stories that resonate?
- Am I just speaking about the features and how your solution works? Or am I highlighting the outcomes customers care about?
- Can a prospect immediately see WHAT action they need to take on the page and WHAT emotional outcome they will get?
- Am I using relevant social proof that directly dismantles their top 3 concerns/hesitations? Or is my social proof generic?
- Does the page use easy-to-follow design cues? (Is the use of color in CTAs and highlighted elements consistent?)

Sometimes, the answers to the questions above will be easy. Other times, you might need to look for other cues that your messaging strategy isn't quite adding up. Below, you'll get a breakdown of the top copy and design mistakes you can use to diagnose the problem.

HOW TO AUDIT MESSAGING THROUGH AN EMOTIONAL TARGETING LENS

Once you've audited your customer journey, the next step is to look at messaging and design. There are three indicators that typically signal your copy can be optimized to better connect with your customers.

Indicator #1: Your copy came after design
I'm always amazed by how often I see designers create wireframes with lorem ipsum text and then send it to a copywriter or the CRO manager to fill in the blanks. Designing first is a clear sign the customer wasn't the focus when creating the page. The designer created it based on what looks best, what's cool right now or what competitors are doing.

To ensure you stay customer-first, you should ALWAYS write the copy first. The research you compiled in the previous chapters should dictate where testimonials go and how many sentences are required to convey the message. This should NOT be determined by how many sentences or testimonials the designer allows you.

If you know your copy was written after design, regardless of your amazing research insights, your customers will struggle to see themselves on the page. Your copywriter should create the content and then wireframe it so the designer can see what goes where. The designer isn't free to pepper the page with visuals where it looks nice. Every decision should be strategic.

Indicator #2: You're keeping it short for the sake of it
It's become a painful trend in B2B to keep copy as short as humanly possible. Marketers insist that 'people don't read,' but the reality is that people read when you give them a reason to.

Everything on your page should be about your customer. Every feature and description should have an emotional, desired outcome attached to it. Naturally, this is going to make your copy longer.

Reducing words for the sake of keeping pages short creates a problem for your readers. It prevents them from seeing themselves and how they want to feel on the page. And that makes it harder for them to convert. On top of that, short copy keeps you looking like everyone else. If comments like "Can we shorten this a little?" and "Can we say this in fewer words?" are common feedback from your team, that's a clear sign that your team isn't aligned on what to say to your customers — and HOW. *(Your Customer Compass will be a gamechanger here!).*

Indicator #3: You're not making it about the customer
If you don't attach an emotional outcome to what you sell, everyone on your team ends up selling something different. Your ads are different from your landing page, and the emails you send have nothing to do with your ads. Everything becomes disjointed because everyone's speaking to different people.

When you create emotionally resonating pages and emails, prospects can clearly see themselves on the page and convert.

One formula our team often uses when writing copy that connects with the customer is to combine a feature with the emotional outcome the audience desires. For example, you might think your audience cares about automated invoicing, but when you dig deeper, you find what they really care about is eliminating the time they waste chasing payments. In the table below, you'll see examples of what happens when you shift the focus from the surface-level function to the deeper goal behind it when talking about your product features. If the way you talk about features in your marketing reads more like the copy in the first column, it's time to do something about it.

You're making it about you	You're making it about the customer
Cloud storage and backup	Relax knowing all your critical data is protected with cloud storage and backup
Real-time analytics dashboard	Make informed decisions with real-time analytics
Profitability Report	Be profitable. Always. See which projects are performing and make data-driven decisions that grow the profit margin with a profitability report you can count on.
All-in-one platform	Never wonder 'Do we have the resources to handle this?', 'Who's responsible for delivering that?' or 'Is this project profitable?' again. All the answers will be on one platform. Always.

HOW TO AUDIT DESIGN THROUGH AN EMOTIONAL TARGETING LENS

In optimization, most people will look at the copy and leave it there. However, your design is just as important for creating a customer experience that helps customers buy. There are three indicators you can look for to help you identify key areas for optimization.

Indicator #1: Your images don't support your messaging

When people look at the image in your hero section, they should instantly feel seen and intrinsically understand what you're promising them.

If your big promise is that your product will help your reader get a promotion, the accompanying image should convey the excitement of getting that promotion. Most B2B companies just use screenshots of their product, but that's because they don't know how to leverage images strategically. The problem is that no one cares (yet) what your product looks like, and every halfway decent platform looks the same. If you're going to show images of your product, the images need to be connected to the outcomes your customer wants. For example, when one of our clients shows a screenshot of their profitability report on a page, it's because they're showing their ICP how easy it is to see what everyone on the team is doing. The screenshot isn't isolated—it's thoughtfully integrated with the surrounding copy to tell a complete story. The screenshot is relevant to that specific section on the page and the problem the ICP needs solving.

Indicator #2: Emotions aren't used consistently throughout the customer journey

Every element of your design, from the colors and images to the shape of the call to action button, should reflect where customers are emotionally. Randomly adding an animation of faceless triangle people or a stock photo of a team on their laptops will not help you connect with your customers. You need to think strategically about how you're using design and why.

While working on optimizing iPhone Life's sales page, one of the first things we did was test swapping out the screenshot of the membership site for an image of a customer in his 50s, happily using his device. This was one of the key changes that led to the 18% uplift they saw on that page — because now the customer could easily see the promised outcome reflected on the page

Indicator #3: It's unclear what action people need to take to get what they want
Your design should help prospects take the next step and understand what they need to do next to achieve the emotional results they're looking for. Just as much as copy and design, your UX has an emotional impact on your prospects.

Sometimes, you can get a conversion uplift simply by swapping out your CTA for the action your customers want to take. While best practices recommend "get a demo" as a CTA because it's outcome-focused, I've seen companies increase their conversions by replacing their buttons with 'Contact Sales' because they wanted to talk to a human being.

Emotional targeting case study: How a B2B company increased ICP sign-ups by focusing on the journey, not the destination

The navigation menu is one of the most important parts of any website — it's how prospects get to the information they need to see to convert. Because of that, too many businesses pack the nav with every link in existence (or what they've seen other brands do). They're trying to deliver everything *they think* a prospect might possibly wish to know, instead of using it to guide prospects to the most important information *they're* actually looking for..

So when GetUplift partnered with a B2B project management solution company to help them optimize their user journey, we paid particular attention to the menu.

The existing menu was long and extensive—serving up every feature page, use case, solution page, and add-on page. This wealth of information obscured the pages customers actually needed to make informed decisions. During our A/B tests, we leveraged conversational copy that guided prospects toward the product tour page, integrations, customer stories, and several specific feature pages. Since we knew prospects were comparing them to other solutions as part of the decision-making process, we also included a direct callout to comparison pages.

These changes helped prospects get to places quicker, leading to more clicks, longer time on the website and a lower bounce rate. And it helped **increase ICP signups by 6%.**

WRAPPING UP YOUR AUDIT

Once you've completed your audit, you should be able to identify potential areas for optimization based on the questions you answered 'no' to. For example, if you're not using relevant social proof that directly dismantles your ICP's top three concerns/hesitations, or you have the exact same logos on every page regardless of whether they're connected to the content or not, you now have an opportunity to incorporate social proof in a more strategic way.

In the next chapter, we'll talk about how to use your audit to create a hypothesis that gets the whole team on the same page and allows you to create meaningful tests that actually get meaningful (and measurable) results.

CHAPTER 7

RUNNING MEANINGFUL TESTS

IRON MAN'S SUIT DIDN'T WORK ON THE FIRST TRY. GREAT MARKETING DOESN'T EITHER. BUILD. TEST (STRATEGICALLY). REFINE. REPEAT.

> "I'm not going to stop the wheel, I'm going to break the wheel."
> - Daenerys Targaryen *(without the burning the world part)*

It's time to permanently step off the deadly hamster wheel of optimization and replace it with meaningful strategy

After synthesizing your research, you'll have some very strong ideas about the messages and designs that will resonate with your audience. But here's the challenge: no matter how much emotion-focused research you do, you can never be 100% sure how well your messaging will resonate until you put it out there. **This is why we test.**

The problem is that the minute you introduce a new test, everyone and their neighbor's cat bombard you with opinions. When this happens, tests get diluted, results shrink and frustration rises for the CRO team *(that once again didn't get to test what they wanted)* and for the executive team *(that isn't seeing the results that they need and want 'bigger bets')*.

To escape this trap, use the findings from your research and audit to create testing hypotheses on what will resonate with your audience.

You'll use your hypotheses to:

- Make sure everyone understands and agrees on the goal of the test
- Create a more productive relationship and eliminate opinion-based, back-and-forth feedback
- Get better results from your copywriters, designers and developers because they'll understand why they're doing what they're doing

- Sell tests internally to your executive team because you can back each theory with data and meaningful insights
- Build a clear roadmap for testing so you always know what comes next

Here's the best part — the Customer Compass makes it easy to create effective testing hypotheses.

WHAT MAKES A STRONG HYPOTHESIS

Let's begin by defining what a strong hypothesis is not. A strong hypothesis is NOT recommending that because your competitor added a carousel, you should follow industry standards and it will increase conversions. **A strong hypothesis is always based on a problem and sets out to solve it.**

During your audit, you identified a list of problems that need to be addressed. For instance, prospects might not immediately realize that the solution is specifically designed for them. You hypothesize that clearly communicating who the product is for and how it helps will boost conversions. That's a strong hypothesis. You'll then pair that hypothesis with a practical suggestion of how to test it.

You don't have to come up with all the answers on your own. Once you have your hypothesis, you can give the rest of your team the opportunity to present their ideas. Your designer, for example, might have an idea of how to visually communicate that the tool was built to solve a specific problem. Because everyone is working under the same hypothesis, tests will feel aligned with the high-level strategy work you're doing.

Should you present a hypothesis to key stakeholders, it's helpful to share a slide deck. This should include customers' quotes and data so everyone can see the actual research behind the testing theory. This helps get everyone on board with your hypothesis. Maybe they'll have some feedback, but they won't question your ideas because they will see that they're rooted in quantifiable research.

Once everyone agrees on the problem that needs fixing, and on the roadmap to fixing it, the next step is to create a brief. This is where you get more detailed and share what you're going to do next — e.g., add more specific testimonials, change the headline copy and switch the image in the hero section. You're essentially mapping out everything you're changing, whether it's a full page or just a headline.

This is the right order because it ensures that anyone who jumps into this brief (be it a new hire, an exec or a consultant) can first immediately see the WHY behind your test. This is crucial because it helps you center the conversation around the problem you're trying to solve and the path to doing so — instead of getting stuck in the details.

IDEAS FOR MEANINGFUL TESTS YOU CAN RUN

Meet the three most impactful emotion-based tests we run for our clients. Use these as a starting point for your hypothesis-building.

Test #1: Pains vs desired outcomes

One of our favorite emotion-based experiments involves testing the customer's current pain against their desired emotional outcome to see which resonates more.

To execute, you'll need to create two variations for your page. One variation should primarily focus on the pains, struggles, and challenges you uncovered in your research. The other should focus on how they're going to feel and what they're going to achieve.

Note that in both variations, you'll probably include the pain and the outcome because you can't talk about the pain and get them to convert without promising a solution. Equally, you can't talk about solutions without stating what problem you're solving. The goal of both variations is to show customers you understand them. The focus on pains vs. desired outcomes is what changes.

For example, we've run this test for several of our clients, including a mattress company. We tested the primary desired outcome against the primary pain point in the headline of the home page to see which resonated more.

Variation One (Desired Outcome)	Variation Two (Current Pain)
SLEEP LIKE YOU'RE ON VACATION Sink into this soft, comfortable mattress every night. You deserve it!	YOU NEED A GOOD NIGHT'S SLEEP. EVERY NIGHT. Tossing and turning can be a thing of the past. Treat yourself to a mattress that supports your body.

A test like this will help you uncover what types of messages resonate most with your audience. If you discover that the problem they need solving motivated most of your ideal customers, you can then apply this to other steps in your funnel.

Test #2: Product- vs. customer-focused

This next test is ideal if you're a VP, marketing leader or CMO and know that it's going to be a struggle to get the rest of your team onboard with new experiments.

The test is simple:

You test your current strategy (which is solution-focused) against a new strategy that is customer-focused. What you're doing here is adding emotional outcomes to the existing copy. You're not rewriting or redesigning everything. You're taking one piece like a header or a landing page, and instead of it saying 'the all-in-one platform for X,' it will express the emotional outcome your ideal customers are looking for.

This is a great way to start testing people's responses when you make the page about them. You don't even have to change your headline. You could simply change some bullet points where you call out specific features and marry them with the emotional results.

You can test the customer-focused approach anywhere. You could start by writing a handful of emails that are focused on the customer and see how people respond. If the response is positive, you now have evidence that the customer-focused approach works for your brand, and you can start applying the principle to other parts of your funnel.

Below, you'll see an example of how HubSpot could switch its headline to be more customer-focused. The first variation could describe any chat software and pretty much any SaaS company. There's no differentiator here.

Variation One: Solution-focused	Variation Two: Customer-focused
LIVE CHAT SOFTWARE Connect with your website visitors in real time to convert new leads, close more deals and provide better support to your customers.	YOUR PROSPECT'S EXPECTATIONS ARE CHANGING. YOU CAN EXCEED THEM. Deliver seamless support and guidance that leaves your prospects delighted with the power of co-browse and live chat.

The second variation puts the focus on the customers, what they're looking for, and explains how the features help deliver these results.

Test #3 Social vs. self-image

When you synthesized your research in Chapter 5, you began organizing research into buckets based on whether social or self-image motivated the customer. But which do they care more about? This is something you can (and should) test.

Besides headlines, subject lines and ads, another great place to test this is in your testimonials. You can test testimonials that focus on how your solution helped the customer improve their self-image vs. testimonials that talk about the rest of their team. You could also test adding both types of testimonials in one variation against the existing solution-focused testimonials (the control).

Variation One: Self-image testimonial	Variation Two: Social-image testimonial
"I felt really confident integrating the software with our current system because the onboarding showed me exactly what to do"	"I'm everyone's new favorite person because I've saved the team around 800 hours of time"

While your audience will probably care about both, some people will care more about one than the other. Once you have evidence of which emotion cluster resonates most, you can start integrating this into your subject lines, ads, emails — and even the hero section of your home page.

HOW TO KNOW IF YOUR TESTING STRATEGY IS WORKING

Strategic testing is about more than celebrating the winners and switching off the losers.

There needs to be a shift in the way you review experiments. Instead of hoping that you'll run a test and quadruple your results, you need to set your mind on learning as much about your customers and prospects as possible so you can consistently improve everything. Even if a variation underperforms, that's OK. Because you're still learning. Giants like Amazon, Booking.com, and Air BnB will testify that 8 or 9 out of 10 experiments they run fail because testing is all about finding the best solution to a problem. And that's hard. However, when you have an overarching strategic goal for the whole year and you stop banking on each test individually, you stand to gain a lot more in the long run.

Four ways to determine the success of your CRO program:

1) There's an active, quarterly strategic roadmap you're following that evolves and is optimized as tests launch and end
2) There's a process — you know what you're measuring and when; you know what to test and what not; and you're logging things in a directory

3) There's cross-team collaboration — insights are shared and used by all teams. CRO supports most marketing and growth teams
4) You've set goals to increase CR/metrics throughout the year and you're adapting as you go and as you see results — meaning you may say you want a 5% uplift in free to paid conversions this year, but as you start testing and things evolve, you realise we need to update this %

You do need metrics and KPIs to measure success — and a X% overall uplift is a nice goal, but when CRO is ingrained within all of your marketing strategy, it may be hard to pinpoint what caused that 3% uplift. You won't be working in isolation, so sometimes you'll say you want to see an uplift from X number of experiments but you'll have to take all marketing campaigns and assets into account (e.g., paid, brand, lifecycle etc.). It's no longer just CRO accountable but the entire team.

It's also crucial to remember that **optimization is a continuous process.** It's circular, with each test giving you meaningful insights you can apply in the next iteration. Even if you know the big pain you're trying to solve, it's important to remember that there are multiple ways you can present it on the page. Just because one pain-focused headline underperforms, that doesn't mean you should scratch all the research that suggests this pain should be addressed. You can present the pain as an image or a color and weave it throughout the entire customer journey until it resonates and connects. A test 'failing' doesn't mean you made the wrong decision. It means you have learned useful information about your customers but still have to figure out how to present it in a way that resonates.

There are many indicators that can help you know whether an approach is working. The most obvious is if it's increasing the metric you're measuring. If a variation is improving your signups, it's obviously working, but that's just the beginning. Similarly, there are other signals that what you're doing is resonating — people will tell you. You might start receiving emails from people saying they love your messaging or start getting more mentions on social. You might even get fantastic feedback on your website changes during your ICP interviews.

For example, Strata's brand and personality have become a defining factor in its growth strategy.

"Before GetUplift, we were in the very early stages of developing our messaging and our voice. Now, people are starting to recognize our voice and tone. They're recognizing our brand and our personality has been a defining factor — it flows through to all the different elements.

We're still young and we're still a work in progress but when we go to events and when prospects talk to our sales team, they will say that our voice is very recognizable and comes through as professional but approachable — and not overly serious — but without being too casual. It's not stuffy tech boring."

Heidi King
Content Marketing Strategy & Production Manager, Strata Identity

While not every test will win, if you continue to implement everything you've learned in this book, results will come, and most importantly, experiment insights will help guide your team's strategy, campaigns and future decisions.

So keep testing. Keep iterating. And most importantly, keep your customers at the center of everything you do.

CHAPTER 8

BRINGING IT HOME

A HERO'S WORK IS NEVER DONE. THERE'S ALWAYS ONE MORE MYSTERY TO UNCOVER, ONE MORE PROBLEM TO SOLVE.

Now that you've worked your way through the Emotional Targeting Framework, you finally have an answer to the question you never asked:

How do you sell a skydiving experience to someone who's afraid of heights?

Answer: you don't.

You sell them on the spontaneous, care-free version of themselves that others admire and aspire to be.

This is a pivotal moment in your optimization journey. Pivotal because if someone can persuade a scaredy-cat like me to jump out of a plane, you can persuade your prospects to buy, try and love your solution. It's a matter of connecting the action you want them to take to the emotions that drive them to change their behavior.

Of course, you've also seen that emotional targeting isn't about persuading anyone and everyone to buy from you. Nor is it about manipulating emotions into existence for the sake of the sale. It's about solving problems for your customers and helping them choose you because you've addressed their existing emotional needs. And as we've seen throughout this book, it's painfully difficult for customers to make a decision without engaging their emotions.

I know the shift might feel strange at first, especially if you're operating within a team that's used to dealing exclusively with data. However, I can tell you with near 100% certainty that implementing The Emotional Targeting Framework will feel less painful than staying on the deadly hamster wheel of optimization and not seeing results

– *especially* when you start being responsible for some of the most awesome uplifts the company has ever seen.

So treat your new framework as a means of winning your team over to your new approach to CRO. But also, treat it as a loyal partner that will help you consistently uncover new growth opportunities that everyone is excited to get behind.

And when you're standing in front of an A/B test that bombed *(bound to happen)*, remember that every insight brings you closer to understanding your customers on a deeper emotional level. Every survey, every interview, every test is helping you get closer to showing your customers you "get' them by leaning into the emotions that drive their decisions.

With all that growth-creating knowledge in your pocket, you can permanently stop talking to the building — and start connecting and converting the person inside.

Ready to become the conversion superhero your company needs? Choose from three powerful ways to implement the Emotional Targeting Framework™:

FREE COMPANION WORKBOOK
Unlock your customers' true motivations with Talia's practical workbook. Discover powerful reflective questions that reveal hidden conversion opportunities, see real Customer Compasses that doubled conversions, and get your own roadmap off the deadly hamster wheel of optimization.

EMOTION SELLS: THE INTENSIVE
Like a superhero training academy, The Intensive equips growth-minded marketing teams with everything needed to master emotional targeting. Access every tool, resource, and slide deck to implement The Emotional Targeting Framework™, plus direct access to Talia Wolf.

DONE FOR YOU CRO SERVICES
When you need the conversion optimization dream team, Talia's GetUplift experts deliver. They help fast-growing, profitable companies execute powerful, customer-first optimization programs. Trusted by brands like Bitly, Amplitude, CatoNetworks, and SproutSocial, the GetUplift team brings their battle-tested methodology to transform your conversions.

Choose your path and start connecting with customers on a deeper emotional level today.

SPEAKING AND KEYNOTES

Talia has taught her methodology on hundreds of global stages. Hire Talia to speak at your conference or company event to give your audience a mix of strategy and practical tactics, grounded in the work Talia and her team do every day *(with all the dull parts cut out).*

For more details on how to book Talia for your next event visit www.taliawolf.com/speaking

ACKNOWLEDGMENTS

I owe so much to many, many people for their direct and indirect support of this book and my career. If there's one thing I'm clear about, it is that I did not get here on my own.

I would not be where I am today if it wasn't for the incredible support, encouragement and occasional *(much-needed)* shoving from my partner in life and best friend, Omri. Thank you for going on this life-long journey with me, for believing in me and for reminding me through every single challenge, that ***"I love you"*** *is always followed by* ***"I know."***

GetUplift and everything I've built wouldn't be what they are today without the person who's been with me from the very beginning—my partner in crime and dear friend, Sophia Dagnon. (And let's be honest, this book would never have seen the light of day if you hadn't pushed me across the finish line.) Thank you for your passion, your commitment, and your unwavering belief in our work. I am beyond grateful to have you by my side—today and always. This business, this book, and this entire adventure wouldn't be the same without you.

To my mum and dad — my greatest teachers and biggest supporters. Thank you for your love and for the daily reminders to believe in myself. Thank you for pushing me to be the best version of myself, and for always reminding me what matters most in life: **Family**. You inspire me more than you'll ever know. This book, like everything I do, carries a piece of you in it.

To my Wolf Pack — Jony, Daniel, and Lee — who've been with me through thick and thin. Thank you for keeping me grounded, for answering the late-night calls, for reminding me to laugh at myself, and for your endless love and support. I'm so grateful to have you by my side.

And of course, to my Shine Crew. Gia Laudi, Tara Robertson, Joanna Wiebe, Tiffany DaSilva, April Dunford, Els Aerts, Krista Seiden, Claire Suellentrop and Angie Schottmuller. You've been with me since Day 1. Thank you for reminding me to take breaks, for celebrating my wins like they were your own, and for always believing in me — even when I doubted myself.

ABOUT TALIA WOLF

Talia Wolf is a conversion optimization specialist and marketing strategist. For more than a decade, some of the biggest brands in B2B, SaaS, Finance, Travel and retail have hired Talia and her team at GetUplift, the CRO agency she runs, to help them improve conversions using The Emotional Targeting Framework. Named one of the most influential speakers and experts in marketing and optimization, Talia's spoken on hundreds of stages and has trained thousands of marketers in her emotion-focused approach to optimization.

When she's not helping marketers become the heroes their companies need, Talia can be found debating the merits of DC versus Marvel universes, analyzing character arcs across different continuities, and drawing parallels between superhero origin stories and customer transformation journeys. Her encyclopedic knowledge of comic lore, from Golden Age classics to modern multiverse storylines, infuses her marketing philosophy with a unique understanding of how emotion drives human decision-making.

Printed in Great Britain
by Amazon